Bible Study for Freemasons

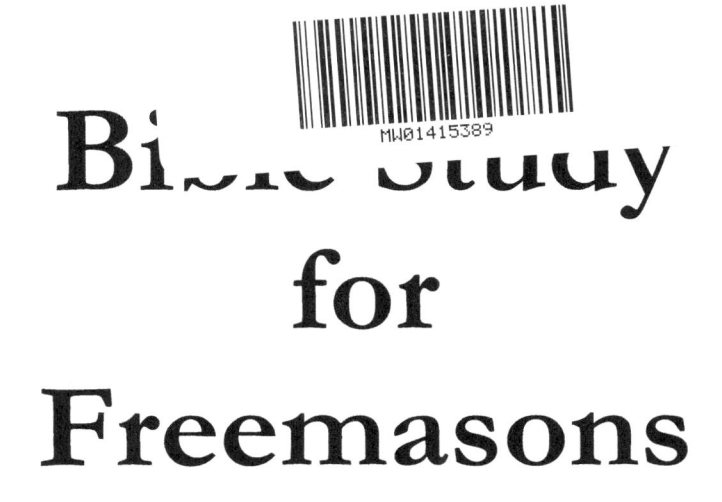

By Dr. Robert J.F. Elsner

Past Master, Clinton Lodge #3 AFM, Abbeville, SC (2007)

District Deputy Grand Master, 11th District,
Grand Lodge AFM of South Carolina (2018-2020)

Grand Commander of Knights Templar of South Carolina (2018-2019)

Bible Study for Freemasons

By Dr. Robert J.F. Elsner

Copyright © 2018 by Robert J.F. Elsner
All rights reserved. No part of this book may be reproduced for any purpose without the express written consent of the author beyond fair use.

ISBN - 9781797553849

Scriptures marked KJV are taken from the KING JAMES VERSION (KJV): KING JAMES VERSION, public domain. Scriptures marked NIV are taken from THE HOLY BIBLE, NEW INTERNATIONAL VERSION®, NIV® Copyright © 1973, 1978, 1984, 2011 by Biblica, Inc.™ Used by permission. All rights reserved worldwide.

This book is dedicated to the
Glory of God
in thanksgiving for the many brothers
who have spurred on my faith development
and my urge to serve God better
through my scholarship and teaching.

All my work, as with all my life, is dedicated to my family.

It is also dedicated to my two colleagues
heading up the York Rite Bodies of South Carolina
with me during the 2018-2019 years,
MEGHP Tony Bizakis and MIGM Jerry Willard.
Thank you, my brothers,
for pushing me to be a better man and mason.

Preface

2 Timothy 3:16-17
[16] All scripture is given by inspiration of God, and is profitable for doctrine, for reproof, for correction, for instruction in righteousness: [17] That the man of God may be perfect, thoroughly furnished unto all good works.

Masonry is a beautiful system of morality, veiled in allegory, illustrated by signs and symbols, and embodying ideals that transcend most human barriers. The work of masonry is based upon and filled with scripture, with beauty, and with God's love, irrespective of any one individual's relationship with God. The one requirement of a man who would like to join masonry is that he believes in God. The problem that some people have with Freemasonry is that we, just like the US Constitution[1], believe that even if we do not agree with someone on their religion, we should be respectful and seek out agreement instead of tension. With declines in church attendance, many young men become masons seeking the divine, but being unwilling to join organized religion. They might say things like "I am spiritual, but not religious." This sometimes arms those who do not understand masonry with weapons of fear, and what we fear, we tend to hate. Some of the most famous masons who helped develop the Craft in the USA also hurt it the most, such as Albert Pike whose passions led him to bluster in words. While his work is amazing in so many ways, his hyperbole sometimes goes to such levels of excess, such as where he describes

---

[1] It is fun to talk to college students who study the Constitution who go on to find Anderson's Constitutions of Freemasonry, where much of the US document comes from. They tend to not be arrogant in thinking they know bad things about Masonry.

Freemasonry as a handmaid to religion (which it is), but then goes on to hyperbolically state that Freemasonry is religion itself (which it is not). Unfortunately, even in a country founded by Masons along masonic principles, many are opposed to Freemasonry because of hearsay or lies from those thrown out for unmasonic conduct. Others have read fantasy novels written about masonry by non-masons who do not know how faithful the organization is. I have heard many proclaim masonry to be incompatible with Christianity for one of two reasons. First, because they read misinformation on the internet, which is unfortunate that they do not discern better. Second, and far more often, because they do not know that Masons are not allowed to ask men to join, so get upset that they are never invited to be part of the group, even though it is due to them never asking to join.

    I am proud to be a Mason. Masonry has helped me improve my prayer life and my focus on the church, even when I struggled with the church and denomination I attended. As an evangelist, I want to hear the blessed name of Jesus on people's lips, but as a Mason, my duty is to help men make those decisions for themselves. This volume is designed to help masons and their families to seek light from scripture, whether they have a church or not, whether they are Christian or not. If I have written these scripture studies well, the readers should walk away from this book being better informed and challenged to read more and more scripture, seeking more about God within their traditions, and be more confident believers. People who are more confident in what they believe can have discussions that do not turn to bad arguments, and are not easily offended. Those who can discuss any topic can best work together and best agree.

    In most instances of this book, I have used the lines from ritual in full context, as too often Masons do not follow through and see where lines come from. At other times, the same Chapter of scripture might contain two or three different passages that are of special import to the Craft, thus are better served integrating them. There are many times when an entire chapter is important to read in order to get one short line that is used in a lecture or prayer or degree.

Since not all masonic traditions use the same scriptures, I have endeavored to select scriptures from various masonic jurisdictions around the world, both in the "Blue Lodges" of the first three degrees and those of the Appendant Bodies. I do not identify which degree or source that each scripture reading comes from, as that is for each mason to learn if they do not immediately recognize the verses.

All scripture used throughout this book is from the King James Version of the Bible unless otherwise noted. There are times when other translations give a better sense of the intentions of why we use the lines in Lodges. It is highly recommended that in any serious study of the Bible, several translations are used. For those interested, there are several websites of note, including BibleHub.com and BibleGateway.com. I often used these two sites to assist in my studies during the construction of this book. If you are interested in Biblical languages, I recommend using the BibleHub.com resources, clicking on Hebrew or Greek to take you to the original languages and helping you see where else each particular word is used as per Englishman's Concordance, Strong's, and several other major reference works.

Where I have translated from Hebrew or Greek, it should be stated that the translations are mine, and any errors made are mine and not those of any source from which I sought assistance. I have tried to be faithful to scripture and modern English (American) language. While I had several brilliant Hebrew professors in both Seminaries I graduated from, my abilities do not show their great skill teaching, only my poor abilities learning. For those of you who read Hebrew, please note that some words are pointed, some not, purely due to typesetting issues, not for any other purpose. You may also note that when whole chapters are used, there are still verse designations except for the Psalms, most of which are used in their entirety. This is strictly for aesthetic purposes of uniformity.

    Several other works informed the discussions here, including The Anchor Bible Series of Commentaries, the Exegetical Guide to the Greek New Testament, the Story of God Bible Commentary, and many others. I have attempted to bring the benefit of scholarship without the burdens thereof so that this book might be easier to read and use. It is worth noting that when most major Bible translation began in the 1500s, it centered in Germany, thus many spelling traditions are German. Among the most important of these to note is that in German, the letter "J" is pronounced as a "Y" in English. This is fine for Germans, as there is no *"J"* sound in Hebrew, so *"Joshua"* would be pronounced correctly as *"Yah-shoo-ah"* for a German or a Jew. This does pick up problems in English, however, where sounds are different, and we can be misled in pronouncing things. Pronunciation is not as important as meaning, but these items are important to help people learn correctly and well.

    When the Reformation began in earnest (remembering that it was underway in England in 1380 with John Wycliffe translating the Bible and teaching peasants scripture), one of the three greatest reformers was Thomas Cranmer. He, Luther, and Calvin are credited not with the ideas, but getting things done. Cranmer had an amazing gift for English language, and his original Book of Common Prayer certainly inspired many poets and theologians. One of the collects from that is appropriate here:

> BLESSED Lord, who hast caused all holy Scriptures to be written for our learning; Grant that we may in such wise hear them, read, mark, learn, and inwardly digest them, that by patience and comfort of thy

holy Word, we may embrace, and ever hold fast, the blessed hope of everlasting life, which thou hast given us in our Saviour Jesus Christ. Amen.

It is my hope that you will use the note spaces in this book to mark and learn as you read so that you can truly inwardly digest the scriptures and sow seeds of truth and beauty into your lives. When I was writing my DMin dissertation, I kept coming across passages from scripture that sang out to me because I knew them so well from Lodge. All too often, however, other brothers did not get the deep meanings as easily, or had learned things poorly in Sunday school (as I had as well…). I wanted to share what I was learning, but not asking everyone to earn their MDiv and DMin degrees to do so.

While I have visited lodges in many countries and US States, I do not claim to be an expert on Masonry. My masonic titles include Right Worshipful, Right Excellent, Right Illustrious, and Right Eminent, but that does not mean I am always right. For the past few years I have been serving in the Elected line of the Grand Commandery of Knights Templar of South Carolina, a part of the York Rite. As the Grand Commander for 2018-2019, I find that the time is right for such bible study to really help make good men better. I have included questions that repeat after each section to focus on making us better men and masons, and hopefully better Christians. My prayers are with the readers of this book that you see these scripture writings are the Word of God, and awaken understanding and love of the Word of God in you.

Rob Elsner
Due West, SC
April 2018

How to use this Book

You might ask what I wrote this book for. The answer is: Several purposes.

First, I wrote it to be an aid to Masons who are not as familiar with the Holy Bible as they would like to be. In this case, study it alone or with a group of people. Bring up these topics at church and delve into your faith in the ways that will help you along your Walk with God.

Second, this book is for those masons who want to integrate the meaning of the words they say and hear in Lodge or in the Appendant Bodies, and need a tiny bit of help to connect the dots.

Third, while all Masons are believers in God, not all are Christian. For those brothers, I hope that this helps explain some of the deeper "shorthand" that Christians use in our scriptural references. While I am Christian, only in cases where it is essential to focus on Christ that I go into the deeper meaning. This was honestly very difficult as an evangelist to not sing His praises, but that is hopefully a subtext that does not offend brothers of other faiths.

Fourth, too often Lodges and other Masonic bodies do not provide appropriate education, so this book might help. Almost all of these study guides are short enough to read the passage and information in Lodge. A couple of them are quite long (c.f., Ruth 1), but need to be so because of the complexity of the passage. If you decide to use this book in that way, and find that you do not recognize any of the lines, remember that it might be a different piece of the puzzle from another Body, or from another Jurisdiction.

Fifth, I wanted to write something that non-Masons can read and see how central the Scriptures are to Masonry. Too often people only hear from uninformed non-Masons, so do not realize how focused on God we are. Lodge is not church, but it is a place where we try to strengthen every Mason's faith in God. The hard part here was to balance this final goal, understanding that anyone can pick this up and read it, with the explanations that would be provided in Lodge where we can single out words or phrases. Thus, all of the material here is in full context whenever possible or appropriate. At times smaller passages are discussed, but these are so common as to not risk anything that would break an obligation.

Finally, it was and is my goal to glorify God through helping all of His image-bearers to be closer to Him. I am a professor and a devout Christian Evangelist. When my words and work can bring people to faith, I feel that my work is worth whatever price I have paid in effort. *Amen.*

Table of Contents

Preface	v
How to use this Book	xi
Old Testament	1
Genesis 1:1-31	3
Genesis 3:1-7	10
Genesis 3:8-24	13
Genesis 4: 16-26	17
Genesis 49:1-33	21
Exodus 3:1-22	27
Exodus 25:1-40	31
Exodus 31:1-11	37
Exodus 35:24 (NIV)	40
Numbers 6:24-26	42
Judges 12:1-15	44
Ruth 1:1-22	48
Ruth 4:1-12	55
1 Samuel 16:1-5	58
2 Samuel 12:24-25	61
2 Samuel 24:16-25 (NIV)	64
1 Kings 5:15-18	67
1 Kings 6: 1-10	69
1 Kings 7:13-51	73
1 Chronicles 3:1-9	78
2 Chronicles 2:1-18	80
2 Chronicles 3:1-17	85

2 Chronicles 4:11-18	88
2 Chronicles 6:12-42	91
2 Chronicles 9:13-28	97
2 Chronicles 36:1-23	100
Ezra 1:1-11	104
Ezra 3:1-13	107
Ezra 4:1-24	111
Ezra 5:1-17	115
Psalm 22	119
Psalm 23	123
Psalm 25	127
Psalm 27	130
Psalm 46	134
Psalm 90	137
Psalm 103:13-22	140
Psalm 115	142
Psalm 118	148
Psalm 121	154
Psalm 122	157
Psalm 133	159
Psalm 141	163
Ecclesiastes 4:1-16	166
Ecclesiastes 12:1-14	169
Isaiah 8:1-10	173
Isaiah 42:1-25	176
Ezekiel 44:1-14	180
Amos 7:1-9	184

Haggai 1:1-11	189
Haggai 2:20-23	192
Zechariah 4:1-14	194
Apocrypha	197
1 Esdras 3 to 1 Esdras 4	198
New Testament	207
Matthew 5:13-16	209
Matthew 6:9-13	212
Matthew 7:1-14	216
Matthew 18:15-20	219
Matthew 20:1-16	223
Matthew 25:21	227
Matthew 28:1-20	231
John 19:1-42	235
1 Corinthians 6:1-11	240
1 Corinthians 13:1-13	243
2 Corinthians 5:1-10	247
2 Thessalonians 3:6-16	251
James 1:17-27	254
1 Peter 2:4-12	258
Revelation 2:12-17	261
Revelation 21:4-6	264
Bible and Masonic Traditions	267
St. John The Baptist and Masonic Tradition	268
St. John The Evangelist and Masonic Tradition	275
Non-Biblical Material of Interest	279
William Shakespeare	280

Hamlet—Act 3, Scene 1:	280
Alexander Pope	283
An Essay on Man: Epistle IV-- Of the nature and state of Man with respect to Happiness	283
Index	287
About the Author	294

Old Testament

Genesis 1:1-31

[1] In the beginning God created the heaven and the earth. [2] And the earth was without form, and void; and darkness was upon the face of the deep. And the Spirit of God moved upon the face of the waters. [3] And God said, Let there be light: and there was light. [4] And God saw the light, that it was good: and God divided the light from the darkness. [5] And God called the light Day, and the darkness he called Night. And the evening and the morning were the first day. [6] And God said, Let there be a firmament in the midst of the waters, and let it divide the waters from the waters. [7] And God made the firmament, and divided the waters which were under the firmament from the waters which were above the firmament: and it was so. [8] And God called the firmament Heaven. And the evening and the morning were the second day. [9] And God said, Let the waters under the heaven be gathered together unto one place, and let the dry land appear: and it was so. [10] And God called the dry land Earth; and the gathering together of the waters called the Seas: and God saw that it was good. [11] And God said, Let the earth bring forth grass, the herb yielding seed, and the fruit tree yielding fruit after his kind, whose seed is in itself, upon the earth: and it was so. [12] And the earth brought forth grass, and herb yielding seed after his kind, and the tree yielding fruit, whose seed was in itself, after his kind: and God saw that it was good. [13] And the evening and the morning were the third day. [14] And God said, Let there be lights in the firmament of the heaven to divide the day from the night; and let them be for signs, and for seasons, and for days, and years: [15] And let them be for lights in the firmament of the heaven to give light upon

Genesis 1:1-31

the earth: and it was so. ⁱ⁶ And God made two great lights; the greater light to rule the day, and the lesser light to rule the night: he made the stars also. ¹⁷ And God set them in the firmament of the heaven to give light upon the earth, ¹⁸ And to rule over the day and over the night, and to divide the light from the darkness: and God saw that it was good. ¹⁹ And the evening and the morning were the fourth day. ²⁰ And God said, Let the waters bring forth abundantly the moving creature that hath life, and fowl that may fly above the earth in the open firmament of heaven. ²¹ And God created great whales, and every living creature that moveth, which the waters brought forth abundantly, after their kind, and every winged fowl after his kind: and God saw that it was good. ²² And God blessed them, saying, Be fruitful, and multiply, and fill the waters in the seas, and let fowl multiply in the earth.

²³ And the evening and the morning were the fifth day. ²⁴ And God said, Let the earth bring forth the living creature after his kind, cattle, and creeping thing, and beast of the earth after his kind: and it was so. ²⁵ And God made the beast of the earth after his kind, and cattle after their kind, and every thing that creepeth upon the earth after his kind: and God saw that it was good. ²⁶ And God said, Let us make man in our image, after our likeness: and let them have dominion over the fish of the sea, and over the fowl of the air, and over the cattle, and over all the earth, and over every creeping thing that creepeth upon the earth. ²⁷ So God created man in his own image, in the image of God created he him; male and female created he them. ²⁸ And God blessed them, and God said unto them, Be fruitful, and multiply, and replenish the earth, and subdue it: and have dominion over the fish of the sea, and over the fowl of the air, and over every living thing that moveth upon the earth. ²⁹ And God said, Behold, I

have given you every herb bearing seed, which is upon the face of all the earth, and every tree, in the which is the fruit of a tree yielding seed; to you it shall be for meat. **30** And to every beast of the earth, and to every fowl of the air, and to every thing that creepeth upon the earth, wherein there is life, I have given every green herb for meat: and it was so. **31** And God saw every thing that he had made, and, behold, it was very good. And the evening and the morning were the sixth day.

The beginning of the First Book of the Bible is among the most well-known statements in all Western languages. The basic idea that the universe itself is a creation of God is central to many faiths, even if those faiths disagree on who God is.

Genesis 1 is, quite literally, the beginning, for not only scripture, but for Freemasonry. Originally called the Hebrew word that opens the Chapter, Beresith, בְּרֵאשִׁית, meaning "In the beginning" or "In beginning," the Greek term became the most common name for this book of the Bible, partly because of the Septaguint, the oldest complete translation of the Hebrew scriptures into Greek, which was the most commonly spoken international language. Among the best known lines of scripture, the opening words of Genesis teach us the ultimate power and unity of God. God was, is, and will be for Himself, not needing anything or anyone except those with whom to share His infinite Love. The reiterated statements of God saying "Let there be" is called the Divine Fiat (fiat means "Let it be"), in which the universe itself came into being at His command. The theological and philosophical term is *creatio ex nihilo*, meaning "creation out of nothing." God does not require materials to work with, as He is the source of all things, all ideas, all energy. Pagan philosophers could not conceive of a time when there was nothing. So this was a radical idea,

Genesis 1:1-31

even though it has been borne out by modern science in such things as the "Big Bang" theory, which reinforces the creation story as told by Genesis. All things came to be through God's Will and in His good order, and the modern cosmologists support the advent and order, even if there are still questions about timing. When Archbishop of Armagh James Ussher (1581-1656) developed the "young Earth" theory that dated all of creation at 6000 years, it was a novel response to new thoughts and sciences. Originally, the young earth theory was an academic exercise on the literality of scripture, yet not to be directly literal in application assigning the date of October 23, 4004BC as the origin of the world, but began to take on a life of its own. The forms of language matter so that they do not destroy faith, but rather build and strengthen it.

  God not only calls things into being, but calls them as they are, not as they were, since they were not in existence until He called them to be. One of the great commentators, Barnes, tells us that God is most often referred to in the plural, אלהים 'ĕlohîym, "Everlasting," which we translate as "God." The noun אלוה ('elôah) or אלה ('eloah) is found in the Hebrew scriptures fifty-seven times in the singular (of which two are in Deuteronomy, and forty-one in the book of Job), and about three thousand times in the plural, of which seventeen are in Job. While many of us who are Christians would see this as an obvious sign and support of the Holy Trinity, it was not taken so before the birth of Christ, but was seen as being the enormity of God.

  An important point in verse two is that the earth was called into being, but not filled with anything, and it was a shapeless mass. Without things in the earth, especially living things, it has no value. It is the living and formed that matter to God in His divine economy (from the Greek words *Oiko-nomia*, meaning rules (*nomos*) of the house (*oikos*), and in the good and proper order necessary for creatures able to image Him—not an image of physical form, but of

Genesis 1:1-31

reason and compassion and love—to be His vice-gerents (helpers who are given authority). Taking dominion is to make decisions for and to be reasonable and loving, ruling and sustaining to build God's Kingdom.

When we recognize the immense power and abilities of God, we are able to begin to recognize the powerful nature of His Love for us: that He created us just to love us. We can do nothing else for Him. Once a human being is able to conceive of a love so awesome that a universe is created solely to share unbounded Love, we can start to see our place and our responsibilities to God and to one another.

In beginning the universe, God did so in six days, each day building upon the preceding day such that an order and plan was laid out. The first day, God created Light. Light might not seem like much, but this is the cosmic idea of Light, both the idea of illumination and the idea of a way of knowing Him. This was enough for one day. The second day, God separated Heaven (order) from the waters (chaos) so that there was a clear idea of what was where and out of what should life come to conquer the idea of chaos. The third day, God separated the waters into layers, and then made earth come forth from the water that had covered it. He then brought forth the various types of plant life. Plants prepared the land for other life, and grew in the glory of God. God then separated light into sun, moon, and stars so that there was Day and Night as we know them. This too was enough for a single day. On the fifth day, God created all of the creatures of the sea, small to great, and then all the creatures that fly in the air. On that sixth day of creation, God created all of the creatures of land, again, from smallest to greatest, ending with a creature that could image Him. At each step, God had pronounced His creation to be good, but humanity he declared to be very good. Humanity was created such that we are the image bearers of God, able to tend and maintain His creation and love it as He loves it. This supreme accomplishment was in setting forth a

Genesis 1:1-31

universe that could receive the enormity of God's Love and potentially love Him back. This great labor demanded rest in order that we could know to follow His example in that too, resting from our labors, but making sure that our labors were good, or even very good.

Questions to ask:

- Which of the words, lines, or ideas do you recognize from Masonic Work? (Remember to not write them down)
- How do these words, lines, or ideas take the meaning of the degrees and Masonic work and focus them to help make our lives more fit for the Builder's purpose and be Good Men and Masons?
- How do these words, lines, or ideas build our Faith in the Great Architect of the Universe?
- Which of these words, lines, or ideas OTHER than what is used in your Masonic jurisdiction help you to maintain your integrity and work for peace and justice?
- Discuss how these lines could be misunderstood or taken for other purposes that do not glorify God or help you grow as Masons.

NOTES:

Genesis 1:1-31

Genesis 3:1-7

¹Now the serpent was more subtle than any beast of the field which the Lord God had made. And he said unto the woman, Yea, hath God said, Ye shall not eat of every tree of the garden? ² And the woman said unto the serpent, We may eat of the fruit of the trees of the garden: ³ But of the fruit of the tree which is in the midst of the garden, God hath said, Ye shall not eat of it, neither shall ye touch it, lest ye die. ⁴ And the serpent said unto the woman, Ye shall not surely die: ⁵ For God doth know that in the day ye eat thereof, then your eyes shall be opened, and ye shall be as gods, knowing good and evil. ⁶ And when the woman saw that the tree was good for food, and that it was pleasant to the eyes, and a tree to be desired to make one wise, she took of the fruit thereof, and did eat, and gave also unto her husband with her; and he did eat. ⁷ And the eyes of them both were opened, and they knew that they were naked; and they sewed fig leaves together, and made themselves aprons.

Many translations of the Bible term the serpent as the "wisest of creatures" in creation. Serpents tend to be patient, and patience is an attribute of wisdom. This passage has been misused by many people and even in many sermons to justify misogyny, or hatred of women. It is often overlooked that Eve was not surprised at the serpent speaking, and obviously understood it to be a wise creature. The snare was in seeing that knowing good and evil, if you are already good as God had pronounced, meant that you have to learn evil. In order to learn evil, the first parents

Genesis 3:1-7

broke one of God's laws and ate of that fruit. What did they learn? The potential for humans to not simply love God and each other wholly and purely, but to see each other as objects, lustfully and exploitatively, which is not as God had made them. Once this recognition of the depravity of humanity was clear, there was no choice but to put together clothing. Eve may not have believed that God, whom she had known to be so loving, could impart such a penalty against them as death, but she did not understand that death in that context was evil, and she did not yet understand evil.

It should be mentioned here that while Adam and Eve wore aprons, this was not the start of Freemasonry[2]. The word can also be translated as loincloth or skirt, or anything that covers the lower regions from view.

Questions to ask:
- Which of the words, lines, or ideas do you recognize from Masonic Work? (Remember to not write them down)
- How do these words, lines, or ideas take the meaning of the degrees and Masonic work and focus them to help make our lives more fit for the Builder's purpose and be Good Men and Masons?
- How do these words, lines, or ideas build our Faith in the Great Architect of the Universe?
- Which of these words, lines, or ideas OTHER than what is used in your Masonic jurisdiction help you to maintain your integrity and work for peace and justice?
- Discuss how these lines could be misunderstood or taken for other purposes that do not glorify God or help you grow as Masons.

---

[2] Please note, while this is a joke here, it is occasionally brought up by some less informed brethren.

Genesis 3:1-7

NOTES:

Genesis 3:8-24

[8] And they heard the voice of the Lord God walking in the garden in the cool of the day: and Adam and his wife hid themselves from the presence of the Lord God amongst the trees of the garden. [9] And the Lord God called unto Adam, and said unto him, Where art thou? [10] And he said, I heard thy voice in the garden, and I was afraid, because I was naked; and I hid myself. [11] And he said, Who told thee that thou wast naked? Hast thou eaten of the tree, whereof I commanded thee that thou shouldest not eat? [12] And the man said, The woman whom thou gavest to be with me, she gave me of the tree, and I did eat. [13] And the Lord God said unto the woman, What is this that thou hast done? And the woman said, The serpent beguiled me, and I did eat. [14] And the Lord God said unto the serpent, Because thou hast done this, thou art cursed above all cattle, and above every beast of the field; upon thy belly shalt thou go, and dust shalt thou eat all the days of thy life: [15] And I will put enmity between thee and the woman, and between thy seed and her seed; it shall bruise thy head, and thou shalt bruise his heel. [16] Unto the woman he said, I will greatly multiply thy sorrow and thy conception; in sorrow thou shalt bring forth children; and thy desire shall be to thy husband, and he shall rule over thee. [17] And unto Adam he said, Because thou hast hearkened unto the voice of thy wife, and hast eaten of the tree, of which I commanded thee, saying, Thou shalt not eat of it: cursed is the ground for thy sake; in sorrow shalt thou eat of it all the days of thy life; [18] Thorns also and thistles shall it bring forth to thee; and thou shalt eat the herb of the field; [19] In the sweat of thy face shalt thou eat bread, till thou return unto the

Genesis 3:8-24

> ground; for out of it wast thou taken: for dust thou art, and unto dust shalt thou return. [20] And Adam called his wife's name Eve; because she was the mother of all living. [21] Unto Adam also and to his wife did the Lord God make coats of skins, and clothed them. [22] And the Lord God said, Behold, the man is become as one of us, to know good and evil: and now, lest he put forth his hand, and take also of the tree of life, and eat, and live for ever: [23] Therefore the Lord God sent him forth from the garden of Eden, to till the ground from whence he was taken. [24] So he drove out the man; and he placed at the east of the garden of Eden Cherubims, and a flaming sword which turned every way, to keep the way of the tree of life.

Some people might read this as the first time when someone was "thrown under the bus" in modern vernacular. Adam knew he did something wrong, and tried to share blame, and Eve responded with the example set for her by her husband, blaming the serpent.

God loved Adam and Eve so much that he provided for them, even in the time of their sin, making them clothes that required the death of some of Adam's animal friends. There are several plays on words here, as Adam's name, meaning "man," is closely related to the words for dirt or dust. Eve's name, meaning life, is almost synonymous with the word mother, since mothers give life to us all.

For many readers, the idea of work is addressed in special forms, as Adam and Eve had jobs in the Garden, tending and taking care. After leaving the Garden, however, it was not just a privilege to work, but a requirement. What is lost is that God was always and is always working for us with the growing of food, maintaining systems and physical laws, and providing help and guidance. Work became, to many people, a four-letter word. If we are to seek to serve God, however, we need to recapture the idea of work being

Genesis 3:8-24

a privilege, as we work for God's glory and the building of His Kingdom. In Lodge, the teachings of becoming the best worker that you can be are tempered by humility such that we do not risk making work become an idol that we worship, or thinking that we are so good at something because of ourselves and our abilities instead of because of God's blessings.

Questions to ask:
- Which of the words, lines, or ideas do you recognize from Masonic Work? (Remember to not write them down)
- How do these words, lines, or ideas take the meaning of the degrees and Masonic work and focus them to help make our lives more fit for the Builder's purpose and be Good Men and Masons?
- How do these words, lines, or ideas build our Faith in the Great Architect of the Universe?
- Which of these words, lines, or ideas OTHER than what is used in your Masonic jurisdiction help you to maintain your integrity and work for peace and justice?
- Discuss how these lines could be misunderstood or taken for other purposes that do not glorify God or help you grow as Masons.

NOTES:

Genesis 3:8-24

Genesis 4: 16-26

[16] And Cain went out from the presence of the LORD, and dwelt in the land of Nod, on the east of Eden. [17] And Cain knew his wife; and she conceived, and bare Enoch: and he builded a city, and called the name of the city, after the name of his son, Enoch. [18] And unto Enoch was born Irad: and Irad begat Mehujael: and Mehujael begat Methusael: and Methusael begat Lamech. [19] And Lamech took unto him two wives: the name of the one was Adah, and the name of the other Zillah. [20] And Adah bare Jabal: he was the father of such as dwell in tents, and of such as have cattle. [21] And his brother's name was Jubal: he was the father of all such as handle the harp and organ. [22] And Zillah, she also bare Tubalcain, an instructer of every artificer in brass and iron: and the sister of Tubalcain was Naamah. [23] And Lamech said unto his wives, Adah and Zillah, Hear my voice; ye wives of Lamech, hearken unto my speech: for I have slain a man to my wounding, and a young man to my hurt. [24] If Cain shall be avenged sevenfold, truly Lamech seventy and sevenfold. [25] And Adam knew his wife again; and she bare a son, and called his name Seth: For God, said she, hath appointed me another seed instead of Abel, whom Cain slew. [26] And to Seth, to him also there was born a son; and he called his name Enos: then began men to call upon the name of the LORD.

There were two lines from Adam and Eve. After Cain killed Abel, there was only one line of heritage for a while, and thus had to be replaced. Cain's line did not worship God for a while, and thus they developed a lot of industries that were focused on glorifying themselves. They developed social structures and farming, music and

Genesis 4: 16-26

metalworking, and other necessities of life outside of God's presence in the Garden. They were not happy, however, as they did not use these skills to glorify God.

The name Cain is identical to the Hebrew word קין (*qyn*) meaning spear, but also can mean "acquisition." Similarly, Abel's name comes from the noun הבל (*hebel*) usually means vapor, breath, in the negative sense of having no substance and being something very close to nothing. This might be due to the lack of offspring, resulting in his life meaning nothing to other people. More importantly is the idea that the word can also mean mourning. Since Abel is the first person to die, this makes even more sense.

It has been speculated by some scholars that when Ecclesiastes 1:18 tells us that "For in much wisdom is much grief: and he that increaseth knowledge increaseth sorrow," it is describing Cain and Abel's story through playing with these words of their names.

For many people, the names of Lamech's sons are lost in translation. Jabal, Jubal, and Tubalcain are all derived from the same word. The root word is a verb (יבל, *yabal*) that means to produce or being carried or dragged along by a greater force. Please remember that Hebrew does not have a "J" sound, but due to the importance of early German scholarship, we tend to translate Hebrew Y sounds as Js, since the two sound alike in German, even if in written form they are obviously different in English.

In Zephaniah 3:10 the word *jabal* is used for the action of the offerings that exiles bring back to worship God: "From beyond the rivers of Cush my worshipers, my scattered people, will bring me offerings (NIV)." Isaiah 23:7 uses the word to describe those who have been carried away to distant lands. In Jeremiah 23:8: "But, The LORD liveth, which brought up and which led the seed of the house of Israel out of the north country, and from all countries whither I had driven them; and they shall dwell in their own land," the word describes the flow of people as if they were a watercourse. This is not far from the meaning when the

Genesis 4: 16-26

word appears in Isaiah 55:12: "For ye shall go out with joy, and be led forth with peace: the mountains and the hills shall break forth before you into singing, and all the trees of the field shall clap their hands."

It is also important to note that the word *jabal* can be thought of as carried away by circumstance, such that there is no control over their own lives, but are poor players who strut and fret upon the stage and are heard no more.[3] Tubalcain, therefore, can be understood as one who was carried away by acquisition and creation, possibly at the expense of forgetting to worship God because of being so intent on the creation of goods that bring glory to the artist (creator) instead of the Creator. Skill is a gift from God, but it needs to be used to serve and glorify God or it becomes a way to create idols, including setting ourselves as the objects of our own worship.

Questions to ask:
- Which of the words, lines, or ideas do you recognize from Masonic Work? (Remember to not write them down)
- How do these words, lines, or ideas take the meaning of the degrees and Masonic work and focus them to help make our lives more fit for the Builder's purpose and be Good Men and Masons?
- How do these words, lines, or ideas build our Faith in the Great Architect of the Universe?
- Which of these words, lines, or ideas OTHER than what is used in your Masonic jurisdiction help you to maintain your integrity and work for peace and justice?

---

[3] William Shakespeare's Macbeth, Act V, scene 5.

Genesis 4: 16-26
- Discuss how these lines could be misunderstood or taken for other purposes that do not glorify God or help you grow as Masons.

NOTES:

Genesis 49:1-33

¹And Jacob called unto his sons, and said, Gather yourselves together, that I may tell you that which shall befall you in the last days.
² Gather yourselves together, and hear, ye sons of Jacob; and hearken unto Israel your father.
³ Reuben, thou art my firstborn, my might, and the beginning of my strength, the excellency of dignity, and the excellency of power:
⁴ Unstable as water, thou shalt not excel; because thou wentest up to thy father's bed; then defiledst thou it: he went up to my couch.
⁵ Simeon and Levi are brethren; instruments of cruelty are in their habitations.
⁶ O my soul, come not thou into their secret; unto their assembly, mine honour, be not thou united: for in their anger they slew a man, and in their selfwill they digged down a wall.
⁷ Cursed be their anger, for it was fierce; and their wrath, for it was cruel: I will divide them in Jacob, and scatter them in Israel.
⁸ Judah, thou art he whom thy brethren shall praise: thy hand shall be in the neck of thine enemies; thy father's children shall bow down before thee.
⁹ Judah is a lion's whelp: from the prey, my son, thou art gone up: he stooped down, he couched as a lion, and as an old lion; who shall rouse him up?
¹⁰ The sceptre shall not depart from Judah, nor a lawgiver from between his feet, until

Genesis 49:1-33

Shiloh come; and unto him shall the gathering of the people be.

¹¹ Binding his foal unto the vine, and his ass's colt unto the choice vine; he washed his garments in wine, and his clothes in the blood of grapes:

¹² His eyes shall be red with wine, and his teeth white with milk.

¹³ Zebulun shall dwell at the haven of the sea; and he shall be for an haven of ships; and his border shall be unto Zidon.

¹⁴ Issachar is a strong ass couching down between two burdens:

¹⁵ And he saw that rest was good, and the land that it was pleasant; and bowed his shoulder to bear, and became a servant unto tribute.

¹⁶ Dan shall judge his people, as one of the tribes of Israel.

¹⁷ Dan shall be a serpent by the way, an adder in the path, that biteth the horse heels, so that his rider shall fall backward.

¹⁸ I have waited for thy salvation, O LORD.

¹⁹ Gad, a troop shall overcome him: but he shall overcome at the last.

²⁰ Out of Asher his bread shall be fat, and he shall yield royal dainties.

²¹ Naphtali is a hind let loose: he giveth goodly words.

²² Joseph is a fruitful bough, even a fruitful bough by a well; whose branches run over the wall:

²³ The archers have sorely grieved him, and shot at him, and hated him:

²⁴ But his bow abode in strength, and the arms of his hands were made strong by the hands of the mighty God of Jacob; (from thence is the shepherd, the stone of Israel:)

Genesis 49:1-33

[25] Even by the God of thy father, who shall help thee; and by the Almighty, who shall bless thee with blessings of heaven above, blessings of the deep that lieth under, blessings of the breasts, and of the womb:
[26] The blessings of thy father have prevailed above the blessings of my progenitors unto the utmost bound of the everlasting hills: they shall be on the head of Joseph, and on the crown of the head of him that was separate from his brethren.
[27] Benjamin shall ravin as a wolf: in the morning he shall devour the prey, and at night he shall divide the spoil.

[28] All these are the twelve tribes of Israel: and this is it that their father spake unto them, and blessed them; every one according to his blessing he blessed them. [29] And he charged them, and said unto them, I am to be gathered unto my people: bury me with my fathers in the cave that is in the field of Ephron the Hittite, [30] In the cave that is in the field of Machpelah, which is before Mamre, in the land of Canaan, which Abraham bought with the field of Ephron the Hittite for a possession of a burying place. [31] There they buried Abraham and Sarah his wife; there they buried Isaac and Rebekah his wife; and there I buried Leah. [32] The purchase of the field and of the cave that is therein was from the children of Heth. [33] And when Jacob had made an end of commanding his sons, he gathered up his feet into the bed, and yielded up the ghost, and was gathered unto his people.

This passage starts with a warning. Ruben, the firstborn who should have inherited everything, was unstable and did not follow the instructions of his father or

Genesis 49:1-33

of God. Other brothers are shown to also be extremely complex people, such as Dan, who is considered a judge over his brothers, but also a snake that bites their heels. Dan's name comes from the verb דין (*din*) meaning to judge, contend, or plead. Verse 18 causes scholars consternation as why it is there, but the two main streams of thought are that it is relating to the snakebite of verse 17 as an example of what Israel needs salvation from, or that it is the author being overcome by the reality of our need for salvation and of God's graciousness in always providing for us.

    In this section of scripture we derive the idea of the banners of each tribe of Israel, although these are not intended as the banners themselves, but descriptors of the sons. It is essential to mention that the tribes of Israel do not all get banners, Levi got no land, but the tribe was set to serve as priests to be taken care of by the other tribes, and Joseph's tribe is split between two of his sons, Ephraim and Manasseh. Manasseh (מנשה) means **to forget**. "And Joseph called the name of the firstborn Manasseh: For God, said he, hath made me forget all my toil, and all my father's house" (Genesis 41:51). Some have questioned why the second of Joseph's sons became a principal tribe, Genesis 41:52 "And the name of the second called he Ephraim: For God hath caused me to be fruitful in the land of my affliction." His name therefore means "*I am twice fruitful.*"

    There are two streams of ideas for the banners. First are the descriptions above put into context as four principal tribes as described in Numbers 2.

> And on the east side toward the rising of the sun shall they of the standard of the camp of Judah pitch throughout their armies
>   Numbers 2:3.
> On the south side shall be the standard of the camp of Reuben according to their armies
>   Numbers 2:10.

Genesis 49:1-33

> On the west side shall be the standard of the camp of Ephraim according to their armies
>> Numbers 2:18
>
> The standard of the camp of Dan shall be on the north side by their armies
>> Numbers 2:25

Judah's banner is pictured as a lion. Ruben's banner can be pictured as a man. Ephraim's banner is an ox, and Dan's banner is an eagle. These allusions can also tie into two great prophesies of the Living Creatures described in the Great Vision from Ezekiel 1:10: "As for the likeness of their faces, they four had the face of a man, and the face of a lion, on the right side: and they four had the face of an ox on the left side; they four also had the face of an eagle." We have this vision reproduced in Revelation 4:7: "And the first beast was like a lion, and the second beast like a calf, and the third beast had a face as a man, and the fourth beast was like a flying eagle." For these reasons the banners we see often are simply these four, building in us a sense of urgency that we need to promote the best qualities of the tribes and live lives of worship that emulate the heavenly creatures in the direct devotion to God.

Questions to ask:
- Which of the words, lines, or ideas do you recognize from Masonic Work? (Remember to not write them down)
- How do these words, lines, or ideas take the meaning of the degrees and Masonic work and focus them to help make our lives more fit for the Builder's purpose and be Good Men and Masons?
- How do these words, lines, or ideas build our Faith in the Great Architect of the Universe?

Genesis 49:1-33
- Which of these words, lines, or ideas OTHER than what is used in your Masonic jurisdiction help you to maintain your integrity and work for peace and justice?
- Discuss how these lines could be misunderstood or taken for other purposes that do not glorify God or help you grow as Masons.

NOTES:

Exodus 3:1-22

¹Now Moses kept the flock of Jethro his father in law, the priest of Midian: and he led the flock to the backside of the desert, and came to the mountain of God, even to Horeb. ² And the angel of the LORD appeared unto him in a flame of fire out of the midst of a bush: and he looked, and, behold, the bush burned with fire, and the bush was not consumed. ³ And Moses said, I will now turn aside, and see this great sight, why the bush is not burnt. ⁴ And when the LORD saw that he turned aside to see, God called unto him out of the midst of the bush, and said, Moses, Moses. And he said, Here am I. ⁵ And he said, Draw not nigh hither: put off thy shoes from off thy feet, for the place whereon thou standest is holy ground. ⁶ Moreover he said, I am the God of thy father, the God of Abraham, the God of Isaac, and the God of Jacob. And Moses hid his face; for he was afraid to look upon God. ⁷ And the LORD said, I have surely seen the affliction of my people which are in Egypt, and have heard their cry by reason of their taskmasters; for I know their sorrows; ⁸ And I am come down to deliver them out of the hand of the Egyptians, and to bring them up out of that land unto a good land and a large, unto a land flowing with milk and honey; unto the place of the Canaanites, and the Hittites, and the Amorites, and the Perizzites, and the Hivites, and the Jebusites. ⁹ Now therefore, behold, the cry of the children of Israel is come unto me: and I have also seen the oppression wherewith the Egyptians oppress them. ¹⁰ Come now therefore, and I will send thee unto Pharaoh, that thou mayest bring forth my people the children of Israel out of Egypt. ¹¹ And Moses said unto God, Who am I, that I

Exodus 3:1-22

should go unto Pharaoh, and that I should bring forth the children of Israel out of Egypt? [12] And he said, Certainly I will be with thee; and this shall be a token unto thee, that I have sent thee: When thou hast brought forth the people out of Egypt, ye shall serve God upon this mountain. [13] And Moses said unto God, Behold, when I come unto the children of Israel, and shall say unto them, The God of your fathers hath sent me unto you; and they shall say to me, What is his name? what shall I say unto them? [14] And God said unto Moses, I AM THAT I AM: and he said, Thus shalt thou say unto the children of Israel, I AM hath sent me unto you. [15] And God said moreover unto Moses, Thus shalt thou say unto the children of Israel, the LORD God of your fathers, the God of Abraham, the God of Isaac, and the God of Jacob, hath sent me unto you: this is my name for ever, and this is my memorial unto all generations. [16] Go, and gather the elders of Israel together, and say unto them, The LORD God of your fathers, the God of Abraham, of Isaac, and of Jacob, appeared unto me, saying, I have surely visited you, and seen that which is done to you in Egypt: [17] And I have said, I will bring you up out of the affliction of Egypt unto the land of the Canaanites, and the Hittites, and the Amorites, and the Perizzites, and the Hivites, and the Jebusites, unto a land flowing with milk and honey. [18] And they shall hearken to thy voice: and thou shalt come, thou and the elders of Israel, unto the king of Egypt, and ye shall say unto him, The LORD God of the Hebrews hath met with us: and now let us go, we beseech thee, three days' journey into the wilderness, that we may sacrifice to the LORD our God. [19] And I am sure that the king of Egypt will not let you go, no, not by a mighty hand. [20] And I will stretch out my hand, and smite Egypt with all my wonders which I will do in the midst thereof:

Exodus 3:1-22

and after that he will let you go. ²¹ And I will give this people favour in the sight of the Egyptians: and it shall come to pass, that, when ye go, ye shall not go empty. ²² But every woman shall borrow of her neighbour, and of her that sojourneth in her house, jewels of silver, and jewels of gold, and raiment: and ye shall put them upon your sons, and upon your daughters; and ye shall spoil the Egyptians.

Verse 4 contains one of the most important comments man says to God in the OT: Here I am (הִנֵּנִי, *hinnênî*). Moses, as Abraham and Jacob previously, listens to God calling him and responds with an acceptance of his duty to listen to God and do as he is told by the Almighty. It is important to note, however, that English can interchange "Here I am" and "Here am I" (see v.4), but not "Here, I am." In Hebrew, "I am" (אֶהְיֶה pronounced *'eh-yeh*- v.14) is a statement of being, so when God says "I am," it is an ultimate statement of eternal being and existence that likes of which does not translate. Holy ground should not have dust from other areas come to it, so shoes are removed. Removal of shoes also allows us to come into contact with the Holy in ways that we can understand and attempt to be in reverence to. When we recognize the holy and open ourselves to the truth that comes from God, we are set free from all of the issues that bind and enslave us, whether they be of other people's making or of our own.

Questions to ask:

- Which of the words, lines, or ideas do you recognize from Masonic Work? (Remember to not write them down)
- How do these words, lines, or ideas take the meaning of the degrees and Masonic work and

Exodus 3:1-22
> focus them to help make our lives more fit for the Builder's purpose and be Good Men and Masons?
- How do these words, lines, or ideas build our Faith in the Great Architect of the Universe?
- Which of these words, lines, or ideas OTHER than what is used in your Masonic jurisdiction help you to maintain your integrity and work for peace and justice?
- Discuss how these lines could be misunderstood or taken for other purposes that do not glorify God or help you grow as Masons.

NOTES:

Exodus 25:1-40

¹And the Lord spake unto Moses, saying, ²Speak unto the children of Israel, that they bring me an offering: of every man that giveth it willingly with his heart ye shall take my offering. ³ And this is the offering which ye shall take of them; gold, and silver, and brass, ⁴ And blue, and purple, and scarlet, and fine linen, and goats' hair, ⁵ And rams' skins dyed red, and badgers' skins, and shittim wood, ⁶ Oil for the light, spices for anointing oil, and for sweet incense, ⁷ Onyx stones, and stones to be set in the ephod, and in the breastplate. ⁸ And let them make me a sanctuary; that I may dwell among them. ⁹ According to all that I shew thee, after the pattern of the tabernacle, and the pattern of all the instruments thereof, even so shall ye make it. ¹⁰ And they shall make an ark of shittim wood: two cubits and a half shall be the length thereof, and a cubit and a half the breadth thereof, and a cubit and a half the height thereof. ¹¹ And thou shalt overlay it with pure gold, within and without shalt thou overlay it, and shalt make upon it a crown of gold round about. ¹² And thou shalt cast four rings of gold for it, and put them in the four corners thereof; and two rings shall be in the one side of it, and two rings in the other side of it. ¹³ And thou shalt make staves of shittim wood, and overlay them with gold. ¹⁴ And thou shalt put the staves into the rings by the sides of the ark, that the ark may be borne with them. ¹⁵ The staves shall be in the rings of the ark: they shall not be taken from it. ¹⁶ And thou shalt put into the ark the testimony which I shall give thee. ¹⁷ And thou shalt make a mercy seat of pure gold: two cubits and a half shall be the length thereof, and a cubit and a half the breadth thereof. ¹⁸ And thou

Exodus 25:1-40

shalt make two cherubims of gold, of beaten work shalt thou make them, in the two ends of the mercy seat. [19] And make one cherub on the one end, and the other cherub on the other end: even of the mercy seat shall ye make the cherubims on the two ends thereof. [20] And the cherubims shall stretch forth their wings on high, covering the mercy seat with their wings, and their faces shall look one to another; toward the mercy seat shall the faces of the cherubims be. [21] And thou shalt put the mercy seat above upon the ark; and in the ark thou shalt put the testimony that I shall give thee. [22] And there I will meet with thee, and I will commune with thee from above the mercy seat, from between the two cherubims which are upon the ark of the testimony, of all things which I will give thee in commandment unto the children of Israel. [23] Thou shalt also make a table of shittim wood: two cubits shall be the length thereof, and a cubit the breadth thereof, and a cubit and a half the height thereof. [24] And thou shalt overlay it with pure gold, and make thereto a crown of gold round about. [25] And thou shalt make unto it a border of an hand breadth round about, and thou shalt make a golden crown to the border thereof round about. [26] And thou shalt make for it four rings of gold, and put the rings in the four corners that are on the four feet thereof. [27] Over against the border shall the rings be for places of the staves to bear the table. [28] And thou shalt make the staves of shittim wood, and overlay them with gold, that the table may be borne with them. [29] And thou shalt make the dishes thereof, and spoons thereof, and covers thereof, and bowls thereof, to cover withal: of pure gold shalt thou make them. [30] And thou shalt set upon the table shewbread before me alway. [31] And thou shalt make a candlestick of pure gold: of beaten work shall the candlestick be made: his shaft, and his branches, his bowls, his knops, and his

Exodus 25:1-40

flowers, shall be of the same. [32] And six branches shall come out of the sides of it; three branches of the candlestick out of the one side, and three branches of the candlestick out of the other side: [33] Three bowls made like unto almonds, with a knop and a flower in one branch; and three bowls made like almonds in the other branch, with a knop and a flower: so in the six branches that come out of the candlestick. [34] And in the candlesticks shall be four bowls made like unto almonds, with their knops and their flowers. [35] And there shall be a knop under two branches of the same, and a knop under two branches of the same, and a knop under two branches of the same, according to the six branches that proceed out of the candlestick. [36] Their knops and their branches shall be of the same: all it shall be one beaten work of pure gold. [37] And thou shalt make the seven lamps thereof: and they shall light the lamps thereof, that they may give light over against it. [38] And the tongs thereof, and the snuffdishes thereof, shall be of pure gold. [39] Of a talent of pure gold shall he make it, with all these vessels. [40] And look that thou make them after their pattern, which was shewed thee in the mount.

In this section, God tells Moses how to build a place of worship, and that it should be made of fine and expensive items, not for their intrinsic value, but so that the people understood how valuable the act of worship itself is. All of the items are not for God's sake, but for humanity's sake, teaching them aspects of God's life with them in terms that they can understand. The items given for the purposes of building the Tabernacle are given in peace and out of gratitude to God, not to appease God as all other religions of that region (and the rest of the world) had always done. God is not a tyrant that must be bought off to keep Him out of our lives, but a vibrant part of our lives who is

Exodus 25:1-40

deserving of honor and worship and love. We worship and honor God in the Tabernacle or Temple, and show how much we are willing to give of ourselves in time and talent to adorn the place of worship and teach the lessons through the beautification. Until the Reformation, most churches were elaborately painted in order to teach lessons of scripture to an illiterate population, but some worried that there was too much risk of breaking the Commandment of graven images being worshipped, so the practice decreased in many houses of worship. Here, there is no risk of a mistake of people worshipping the tabernacle, as they still had the relationship with the living God and knew that it was decorated to praise God and teach them.

    For millennia, humans have adorned places of worship to not only honor God (or gods), but to show how important those places are. In the ancient world, cities were built surrounding temples, as worship was the center of life. This shifted after the Middle Ages, and towns grew up around economic engines like plants and factories, as that was how people started worshipping things other than God. Now we build around health care centers, as we are at the point of worshipping ourselves and seeing our bodies as the most important part of life, objectifying humanity to so much meat. The body is corruptible and needs to be cleansed of the constant decay.

    It is interesting to note that in the passage above, we see shittim (שטים) wood, also called acacia, as being integral to the construction of the Tabernacle. Acacia is held as a religious wood, since it is one of the only woods that does not rot or decay. The wood is extremely dense and heavy, not very susceptible to insects. It is as close to incorruptible as a wood can be. It is only mentioned in the Bible in connection with the Tabernacle, even though throughout the entire region, it is among the most common of woods. Some have speculated that a particular and very common type of shittim wood, called *acacia raddiana*, was likely the one mentioned in scripture. They are often seen in the

Exodus 25:1-40

desert with their slanted, flat canopies. They conserve water well, but drop all of their leaves in times of severe drought. The roots tend to be very deep, and to extend father than the branches, thus they prevent erosion and are considered good anchors when scaling hillsides. This particular tree also has dense white flowers and coiled seed pods. *(See notes for Exodus 35:24 below.)*

Questions to ask:
- Which of the words, lines, or ideas do you recognize from Masonic Work? (Remember to not write them down)
- How do these words, lines, or ideas take the meaning of the degrees and Masonic work and focus them to help make our lives more fit for the Builder's purpose and be Good Men and Masons?
- How do these words, lines, or ideas build our Faith in the Great Architect of the Universe?
- Which of these words, lines, or ideas OTHER than what is used in your Masonic jurisdiction help you to maintain your integrity and work for peace and justice?
- Discuss how these lines could be misunderstood or taken for other purposes that do not glorify God or help you grow as Masons.

Exodus 25:1-40

NOTES:

Exodus 31:1-11

¹And the LORD spake unto Moses, saying, ²See, I have called by name Bezaleel the son of Uri, the son of Hur, of the tribe of Judah: ³And I have filled him with the spirit of God, in wisdom, and in understanding, and in knowledge, and in all manner of workmanship, ⁴To devise cunning works, to work in gold, and in silver, and in brass, ⁵And in cutting of stones, to set them, and in carving of timber, to work in all manner of workmanship. ⁶And I, behold, I have given with him Aholiab, the son of Ahisamach, of the tribe of Dan: and in the hearts of all that are wise hearted I have put wisdom, that they may make all that I have commanded thee; ⁷The tabernacle of the congregation, and the ark of the testimony, and the mercy seat that is thereupon, and all the furniture of the tabernacle, ⁸And the table and his furniture, and the pure candlestick with all his furniture, and the altar of incense, ⁹And the altar of burnt offering with all his furniture, and the laver and his foot, ¹⁰And the cloths of service, and the holy garments for Aaron the priest, and the garments of his sons, to minister in the priest's office, ¹¹And the anointing oil, and sweet incense for the holy place: according to all that I have commanded thee shall they do.

Some people are called by God to serve Him directly, whereas others do not hear their calling. Moses, Aholiab, and Bezaleel were called directly to serve God and design a new form of worship, igniting the passion for God among His people and teaching them through examples of craftsmanship and artistry. These three serve as archetypes of men working together to serve God, and others like them are repeated again and again in sets of three men who will

Exodus 31:1-11

come together to lead the brothers and sisters of God's people. Moses served in the prophetic capacity, Bezaleel in the construction, and Aholiab in the planning and coordination. Bezaleel, whose name means *"in the shadow of God"* is building something that will provide shadow and protection for the furnishings of worship. Aholiab, whose name means the *"father's tent"* is creating the tent that will be a temporary housing for the worship of God until the Temple is later built by three other men called by God. It is essential to note that this passage reminds us that God provided the talents and abilities needed in these three men, it was not they who brought such to God of their own. In Exodus 36, we find the reminders that these three men oversaw the work using skills God provided, and that the people helped and provided whatever was needed, bringing freewill offerings ever morning what would be needed for that day. God commands and God provides for those commands to be carried out.

Questions to ask:

- Which of the words, lines, or ideas do you recognize from Masonic Work? (Remember to not write them down)
- How do these words, lines, or ideas take the meaning of the degrees and Masonic work and focus them to help make our lives more fit for the Builder's purpose and be Good Men and Masons?
- How do these words, lines, or ideas build our Faith in the Great Architect of the Universe?
- Which of these words, lines, or ideas OTHER than what is used in your Masonic jurisdiction help you to maintain your integrity and work for peace and justice?
- Discuss how these lines could be misunderstood or taken for other purposes that do not glorify God or help you grow as Masons.

Exodus 31:1-11

NOTES:

Exodus 35:24 (NIV)

²⁴ Those presenting an offering of silver or bronze brought it as an offering to the Lord, and everyone who had acacia wood for any part of the work brought it.

In Genesis 25 above, we focused on the tabernacle and the idea of acacia (shittim) wood. In this passage we are told that silver and bronze were brought for offerings. Some did not have these precious metals to give, so instead brought shittim that was needed. The lesson here is that God accepts gifts that are honestly and humbly offered. He does not ask for more than can be given, and God provides for us what we would give to Him. Willing hearts are more valuable than large purses.

This section also points out that all people gave, including both men and women, rich and poor. All were eager to provide what was needed for the worship of God, and worship in a way that seemed worthy, even if that was not the point.

Questions to ask:
- Which of the words, lines, or ideas do you recognize from Masonic Work? (Remember to not write them down)
- How do these words, lines, or ideas take the meaning of the degrees and Masonic work and focus them to help make our lives more fit for the Builder's purpose and be Good Men and Masons?
- How do these words, lines, or ideas build our Faith in the Great Architect of the Universe?
- Which of these words, lines, or ideas OTHER than what is used in your Masonic jurisdiction help you

Exodus 35:24 (NIV)
to maintain your integrity and work for peace and justice?
- Discuss how these lines could be misunderstood or taken for other purposes that do not glorify God or help you grow as Masons.

NOTES:

Numbers 6:24-26

²⁴ The LORD bless thee, and keep thee:
²⁵ The LORD make his face shine upon thee, and be gracious unto thee:
²⁶ The LORD lift up his countenance upon thee, and give thee peace.

This passage is the Aaronic Blessing, where God ordered Moses to have Aaron bless the Children of Israel with these words. It is a blessing of hope and comfort that is cherished by most who hear this blessing sung or said.

Some Christian scholars have taken these words to be a foreshadowing of the doctrine of the Holy Trinity, where verse 24 alludes to God the Father blessing and protecting His chosen people. Verse 25 then would allude to God the Son, whose face actually shined on the people and redefined grace and graciousness. Finally, verse 26 alludes to God the Holy Spirit, who is the great Comforter who brings peace to all.

Questions to ask:
- Which of the words, lines, or ideas do you recognize from Masonic Work? (Remember to not write them down)
- How do these words, lines, or ideas take the meaning of the degrees and Masonic work and focus them to help make our lives more fit for the Builder's purpose and be Good Men and Masons?
- How do these words, lines, or ideas build our Faith in the Great Architect of the Universe?
- Which of these words, lines, or ideas OTHER than what is used in your Masonic jurisdiction help you

Numbers 6:24-26

to maintain your integrity and work for peace and justice?
- Discuss how these lines could be misunderstood or taken for other purposes that do not glorify God or help you grow as Masons.

NOTES:

Judges 12:1-15

[1]And the men of Ephraim gathered themselves together, and went northward, and said unto Jephthah, Wherefore passedst thou over to fight against the children of Ammon, and didst not call us to go with thee? we will burn thine house upon thee with fire. [2]And Jephthah said unto them, I and my people were at great strife with the children of Ammon; and when I called you, ye delivered me not out of their hands. [3]And when I saw that ye delivered me not, I put my life in my hands, and passed over against the children of Ammon, and the LORD delivered them into my hand: wherefore then are ye come up unto me this day, to fight against me? [4]Then Jephthah gathered together all the men of Gilead, and fought with Ephraim: and the men of Gilead smote Ephraim, because they said, Ye Gileadites are fugitives of Ephraim among the Ephraimites, and among the Manassites. [5]And the Gileadites took the passages of Jordan before the Ephraimites: and it was so, that when those Ephraimites which were escaped said, Let me go over; that the men of Gilead said unto him, Art thou an Ephraimite? If he said, Nay; [6]Then said they unto him, Say now Shibboleth: and he said Sibboleth: for he could not frame to pronounce it right. Then they took him, and slew him at the passages of Jordan: and there fell at that time of the Ephraimites forty and two thousand. [7]And Jephthah judged Israel six years. Then died Jephthah the Gileadite, and was buried in one of the cities of Gilead. Ibzan, Elon,

Judges 12:1-15

and Abdon ⁸And after him Ibzan of Bethlehem judged Israel. ⁹And he had thirty sons, and thirty daughters, whom he sent abroad, and took in thirty daughters from abroad for his sons. And he judged Israel seven years. ¹⁰Then died Ibzan, and was buried at Bethlehem. ¹¹And after him Elon, a Zebulonite, judged Israel; and he judged Israel ten years. ¹²And Elon the Zebulonite died, and was buried in Aijalon in the country of Zebulun. ¹³And after him Abdon the son of Hillel, a Pirathonite, judged Israel. ¹⁴And he had forty sons and thirty nephews, that rode on threescore and ten ass colts: and he judged Israel eight years. ¹⁵And Abdon the son of Hillel the Pirathonite died, and was buried in Pirathon in the land of Ephraim, in the mount of the Amalekites.

While at first glance this event seems like a truly barbaric action about property ending the lives of 42,000 people, it is more about protection of the sacred and serious obligations of Israel to God. Ephraim, one of Joseph's sons, was highly blessed in Genesis 48:20, but later turned away from God. Later, the Tribe (Ephraimites) and City of Ephraim are discussed as having lost faith (Hosea7:8, Isaiah 9:21, etc) and worshipping Baal (Hosea 13:1). The real story is a brother leading his family and tribe to become selfish and breaking themselves off from the rest of their people, their family. The Ephraimites became concerned with the worldly and lost sight of the eternal. There would have been pain for the Israelites to hear the Ephraimites speak only of material possessions, as it is for some of us today to hear people only worship power and money instead of God.

    The men of Ephraim were not following God, thus saw life as a burden. The words *"Shibboleth"* (שבלת), meaning the kind of plenty we see in a flowing stream or an

Judges 12:1-15

ear of grain and "*Sibboleth*" (סבלת), meaning burdens or servitude, reflected not only the idea of dialect, but of intention. The words they saw are, in a way, how they view life and faith in God. The Israelites following Jephthah were still worshipping God, thus spoke of His blessings. The Ephraimites no longer worshipped God but still wanted all of the benefits of being part of the people of Israel. Among the most well-known of the passages of Judges, the idea of the word shibboleth as a password has been held by countless people as an indication of knowledge-based salvation instead of faith-based. Early Christians used the term *Shibboleth* as a reminder to each other that God's love of us does not depend upon a particular word and how it is pronounced, but rather is simply a gift from God that none of us are worthy of, yet He freely bestows. Love flows from God, it is not a burden. This is the central point of the passage, that our lives are sometimes summed up by what we say—Faith in God is not a burden, but a liberation that provides for us, and provides richly.

Questions to ask:
- Which of the words, lines, or ideas do you recognize from Masonic Work? (Remember to not write them down)
- How do these words, lines, or ideas take the meaning of the degrees and Masonic work and focus them to help make our lives more fit for the Builder's purpose and be Good Men and Masons?
- How do these words, lines, or ideas build our Faith in the Great Architect of the Universe?
- Which of these words, lines, or ideas OTHER than what is used in your Masonic jurisdiction help you to maintain your integrity and work for peace and justice?

Judges 12:1-15

- Discuss how these lines could be misunderstood or taken for other purposes that do not glorify God or help you grow as Masons.

NOTES:

Ruth 1:1-22

¹Now it came to pass in the days when the judges ruled, that there was a famine in the land. And a certain man of Bethlehemjudah went to sojourn in the country of Moab, he, and his wife, and his two sons. ² And the name of the man was Elimelech, and the name of his wife Naomi, and the name of his two sons Mahlon and Chilion, Ephrathites of Bethlehemjudah. And they came into the country of Moab, and continued there. ³ And Elimelech Naomi's husband died; and she was left, and her two sons. ⁴ And they took them wives of the women of Moab; the name of the one was Orpah, and the name of the other Ruth: and they dwelled there about ten years. ⁵ And Mahlon and Chilion died also both of them; and the woman was left of her two sons and her husband. ⁶ Then she arose with her daughters in law, that she might return from the country of Moab: for she had heard in the country of Moab how that the LORD had visited his people in giving them bread. ⁷ Wherefore she went forth out of the place where she was, and her two daughters in law with her; and they went on the way to return unto the land of Judah. ⁸ And Naomi said unto her two daughters in law, Go, return each to her mother's house: the LORD deal kindly with you, as ye have dealt with the dead, and with me. ⁹ The LORD grant you that ye may find rest, each of you in the house of her husband. Then she kissed them; and they lifted up their voice, and wept. ¹⁰ And they said unto her, Surely we will return with thee unto thy people. ¹¹ And Naomi said, Turn again, my daughters: why will ye go with me? are there yet any more sons in my womb, that they may be your husbands? ¹² Turn again, my daughters, go your way; for I am too old to have an husband. If I should say,

Ruth 1:1-22

I have hope, if I should have an husband also to night, and should also bear sons; **13** Would ye tarry for them till they were grown? would ye stay for them from having husbands? nay, my daughters; for it grieveth me much for your sakes that the hand of the LORD is gone out against me. **14** And they lifted up their voice, and wept again: and Orpah kissed her mother in law; but Ruth clave unto her. **15** And she said, Behold, thy sister in law is gone back unto her people, and unto her gods: return thou after thy sister in law. **16** And Ruth said, Intreat me not to leave thee, or to return from following after thee: for whither thou goest, I will go; and where thou lodgest, I will lodge: thy people shall be my people, and thy God my God: **17** Where thou diest, will I die, and there will I be buried: the LORD do so to me, and more also, if ought but death part thee and me. **18** When she saw that she was stedfastly minded to go with her, then she left speaking unto her. **19** So they two went until they came to Bethlehem. And it came to pass, when they were come to Bethlehem, that all the city was moved about them, and they said, Is this Naomi? **20** And she said unto them, Call me not Naomi, call me Mara: for the Almighty hath dealt very bitterly with me. **21** I went out full and the LORD hath brought me home again empty: why then call ye me Naomi, seeing the LORD hath testified against me, and the Almighty hath afflicted me? **22** So Naomi returned, and Ruth the Moabitess, her daughter in law, with her, which returned out of the country of Moab: and they came to Bethlehem in the beginning of barley harvest.

+++

Quite often, words in the rituals or degrees in Masonry come directly from the King James Version of the

Ruth 1:1-22
Bible. For most Masons, reading through the King James Version of the Bible does not make as much sense as it should. This is not only because of the use of archaic language, or that we don't have the cultural context, but because we stopped thinking about names as functions. Almost all people who appear in the Bible have names that tell us essential information about them: Their character, their job or function in the story, etc. We don't understand the "shorthand" that is so often used in scripture, as we are supposed to know what certain phrases mean, similar to if we said "We the People" to an American versus to someone from an impoverished nation that did not speak English and knew nothing about America. To get the most out of this article, it would be wonderful to have you read the first chapter of Ruth directly from the King James, so that you are reminded of the words you are used to hearing, but also to as yourself how much you really understand.

Before we start looking at the names, let's contextualize this particular chapter from a book that is so important to the First Degree. The first reference in the Book of Ruth is to the Book of Judges. The central theme of that book is in Judges 21:25, which tells us that "In those days there was no king in Israel: every man did that which was right in his own eyes." Faith in God was faltering, and people did not realize that God is the King. They wanted earthly authority, and the Temple was not yet built, so some Israelites strayed from the faith in God. Remember that Israel means *"to struggle with God."* If you were to go and read Ruth 1 right now before reading the rest of this article, it might make a change in your perception. Let's look at the names in this story and then revisit it.

Elimelech is a name that means *"God Is King."* He had been a man of faith, but his faith was starting to wander. He marries Naomi (which means *"My delight"* or *"Sweetness"*) and has two Sons- Mahlon, meaning *"Sickly"* or *"Great Infirmity"* and Chilion, meaning *"Wasting Away,"* *"Pining,"* or *"Consuming."* The sons are called "Ephrathites," which means *"fruitful"* in some places, but means *"worthless"* in this context. Think about common terms like "Buddy," which can either be a great term (Hi Buddy! Good to see you!) or a pejorative (Listen here, Buddy!). Mahlon marries Ruth (meaning "friend" or "companion"); Chilion marries Orpah (meaning "*Neck*" or "*Mane*"- ideals of beauty and luxury). They leave Bethlehem (which means "House of Bread") and go to Moab (which means something to the effect of: "*Who is your Father?*" or in the vernacular: "*Whose your daddy?*"), which is really asking if people believe in God and His sovereignty. When the sons die (Ruth 1:20), Naomi changes her name to Mara (*Bitterness*). Again, reading the King James might help with opening your eyes to what we tend to miss before reading this chapter as I have translated (actually transliterated) it.

+++

¹Now it came to pass in the days when every man did that which was right in his own eyes, there was a famine. And a certain man left the House of Bread where God is Praised, to go to the land where people question who their Father is. ²And the name of the man had been "God Is King," and his wife was named "My Delightful Sweetness," and their two sons "Sickly" and "Wasting Away," who were worthless men. And they came into the country where people question who the Father is, and stayed there. ³And Delightful Sweetness's Praise of God died; and she was left with her two sons, who took wives. ⁴One married Luxury, and the other married a good companion and they lived there about ten years. ⁵Sickly and Wasting Away both died. ⁶Then Sweetness heard that the LORD had visited his people back home and gave them bread in the House of Bread where God is Praised. ⁷They went on the way to return unto the land where God is Praised. ⁸And Sweetness told her two daughters in law, "Go, return to your mother's houses: I pray

Ruth 1:1-22

that the LORD will deal kindly with you, as you kindly dealt with the dead, and with me. [9]The LORD grant you peace and new husbands." Then she kissed them; and they cried loudly and wept. [10]And they said, "Surely we will return home with you." [11]And Sweetness said, "go back home, my daughters: why would you go with me? I am too old to have more sons, so I can't give you new husbands. [12]Go home, my daughters, go your way; I am too old to have another husband. If I should say, I have hope, if God Exists and I had a new husband tonight, and bore sons; [13]would you wait for them to grow up and make them your husbands? No, my daughters; I am sorry for your sakes that the hand of the LORD is against me." [14]And they wept again: and Luxury kissed her mother in law and left; but the Good Companion stayed. [15]Sweetness said, "your sister in law went back to her people, and to her gods: go after her." [16]But the Good Companion said, "Don't ask me to be unfaithful: Where you go, I will go; and where you live, I will live: Your people shall be my people, and your God will be my God: [17]Where you die is where I die and be buried: the LORD should take my life if anything but death separates us." [18]Sweetness realized that she could not change her Good Companion's mind, so stopped trying to. [19]The two of them went back to the House of Bread. People saw them and said, "Isn't that Sweetness, My Delight?" [20]And she said "Don't call me sweetness, call me Bitterness: for the Almighty dealt very bitterly with me. [21]I left God full, but He brought me home empty: why then call me Sweetness, seeing the LORD is against me, and the Almighty has taken away so much from me?" [22]So Sweetness who was bitter and her Good Companion, her daughter in law, returned from where people questioned who the Father was to the House of the Bread where God is praised, when it

Ruth 1:1-22

was the beginning of the barley harvest and there was food.

+++

Let's recap this story. A man lost his faith, and he left God and died. His sons and their potential for a future family died. Luxury left when the sweetness turned bitter, but a good companion stayed where she loved someone. She devoted herself to her friend, and through their commitment to one another, came back to faith in God and were spared from famine. This leads later in the story to the family line of God being praised getting restored through spiritual strength.

One of the keys to this story is that people's names change. We gain new names all the time: Brother, husband, father, son, friend, helper, and on and on, and sometimes we might appear in other people's stories with those names instead of the ones our parents called us. We might make agreements and bind ourselves to them, either with a handshake, a contract, or a pledge, such as giving someone your shoe, without which you cannot leave the city and people publicly see you have made a commitment. Sometimes that commitment is to restore the family line of those who proclaim that God is King.

Ruth eventually marries Boaz (which means *Strength*, and here alluding to spiritual strength), who was the son of Rahab (meaning *violence*) the Harlot from Jericho. Just as Ruth helped redeem Naomi to her sweetness of life in worshipping God, Boaz is the Kinsman-Redeemer who redeems the line of Elimelech, the line of people who know that God Is King. Ruth gives birth to Obed (meaning *Servant*). Obed is the father of Jesse (*Husband*, but also means *God Exists*). Their line goes on until Jesus, *Yeshua*, whose name is also his function: **Salvation**.

Ruth 1:1-22

Questions to ask:
- Which of the words, lines, or ideas do you recognize from Masonic Work? (Remember to not write them down)
- How do these words, lines, or ideas take the meaning of the degrees and Masonic work and focus them to help make our lives more fit for the Builder's purpose and be Good Men and Masons?
- How do these words, lines, or ideas build our Faith in the Great Architect of the Universe?
- Which of these words, lines, or ideas OTHER than what is used in your Masonic jurisdiction help you to maintain your integrity and work for peace and justice?
- Discuss how these lines could be misunderstood or taken for other purposes that do not glorify God or help you grow as Masons.

NOTES:

Ruth 4:1-12

¹Then went Boaz up to the gate, and sat him down there: and, behold, the kinsman of whom Boaz spake came by; unto whom he said, Ho, such a one! turn aside, sit down here. And he turned aside, and sat down. ²And he took ten men of the elders of the city, and said, Sit ye down here. And they sat down. ³And he said unto the kinsman, Naomi, that is come again out of the country of Moab, selleth a parcel of land, which was our brother Elimelech's: ⁴And I thought to advertise thee, saying, Buy it before the inhabitants, and before the elders of my people. If thou wilt redeem it, redeem it: but if thou wilt not redeem it, then tell me, that I may know: for there is none to redeem it beside thee; and I am after thee. And he said, I will redeem it. ⁵Then said Boaz, What day thou buyest the field of the hand of Naomi, thou must buy it also of Ruth the Moabitess, the wife of the dead, to raise up the name of the dead upon his inheritance. ⁶And the kinsman said, I cannot redeem it for myself, lest I mar mine own inheritance: redeem thou my right to thyself; for I cannot redeem it.
⁷Now this was the manner in former time in Israel concerning redeeming and concerning changing, for to confirm all things; a man plucked off his shoe, and gave it to his neighbour: and this was a testimony in Israel. ⁸Therefore the kinsman said unto Boaz, Buy it for thee. So he drew off his shoe.
⁹And Boaz said unto the elders, and unto all the people, Ye are witnesses this day, that I have bought all that was Elimelech's, and all that was Chilion's and Mahlon's, of the hand of Naomi. ¹⁰Moreover Ruth the Moabitess, the wife of Mahlon, have I

Ruth 4:1-12

purchased to be my wife, to raise up the name of the dead upon his inheritance, that the name of the dead be not cut off from among his brethren, and from the gate of his place: ye are witnesses this day. [11]And all the people that were in the gate, and the elders, said, We are witnesses. The LORD make the woman that is come into thine house like Rachel and like Leah, which two did build the house of Israel: and do thou worthily in Ephratah, and be famous in Bethlehem: [12]And let thy house be like the house of Pharez, whom Tamar bare unto Judah, of the seed which the LORD shall give thee of this young woman.

In this passage, several things are happening that are lost to many readers. First, this is not simply about a property deal for Elimelech's land, wife, and daughter-in-law. This is about the redemption of a family line, and the family, as named by Elimelech, is the line of those who believe that **God is King** (which is what Elimelech means). In verse one, there is a kinsman who was discussed in Ruth 3:12-13 who is closer in relation to Elimelech than Boaz, but Boaz has the spiritual strength and integrity to champion the cause of God's people. This unnamed kinsman does not want to give up his own inheritance to revive the name of Elimelech, so he relinquishes the rights to the lands of Elimelech. When this unnamed relative relinquishes his rights, he takes off his sandal and gives it to Boaz, indicating that he has given up the right to walk on the ground of Elimelech as Master. Boaz was then able to take the show to the Elders and purchase the land, using the shoe as proof of the purchase. This tradition is not the same as in Deuteronomy 25:9, and it is important to note, since too often people think it is Boaz talking off his shoe. The subtle to us can be hugely obvious to the people who were familiar with these traditions in their day.

Ruth 4:1-12

Questions to ask:
- Which of the words, lines, or ideas do you recognize from Masonic Work? (Remember to not write them down)
- How do these words, lines, or ideas take the meaning of the degrees and Masonic work and focus them to help make our lives more fit for the Builder's purpose and be Good Men and Masons?
- How do these words, lines, or ideas build our Faith in the Great Architect of the Universe?
- Which of these words, lines, or ideas OTHER than what is used in your Masonic jurisdiction help you to maintain your integrity and work for peace and justice?
- Discuss how these lines could be misunderstood or taken for other purposes that do not glorify God or help you grow as Masons.

NOTES:

1 Samuel 16:1-5

[1]Now the LORD said to Samuel, "How long are you going to mourn for Saul, since I have rejected him as king over Israel? Fill your horn with oil and go. I am sending you to Jesse of Bethlehem, for I have selected from his sons a king for Myself." [2]"How can I go?" Samuel asked. "Saul will hear of it and kill me!" The LORD answered, "Take a heifer with you and say, 'I have come to sacrifice to the LORD.' [3]Then invite Jesse to the sacrifice, and I will show you what you are to do. You are to anoint for Me the one I indicate." [4]So Samuel did what the LORD had said and went to Bethlehem. When the elders of the town met him, they trembled and asked, "Do you come in peace?" [5]"In peace," he replied. "I have come to sacrifice to the LORD. Consecrate yourselves and come with me to the sacrifice." Then he consecrated Jesse and his sons and invited them to the sacrifice.

In this text, we find the issues of what it means to come in peace. We rarely answer with a direct assurance and reply, and in scripture this failure to directly reassure is always an indication of something important. Samuel had consecrated Saul King of Israel and had come to love him. TO see that Saul had failed God was painful, and to have to be the person to consecrate a new king would be even more painful to Samuel. Samuel was a prophet, and rarely is a prophet greeted with joy. When a prophet shows up at the city gates, usually there is going to be trouble, or there has already been trouble that is going to be called out. In this case, the trouble was the king.

1 Samuel 16:1-5

Traditionally, "Do you come in Peace" (בוֹאֲךָ שָׁלֹם) is answered directly as "I come in peace," not "peaceably have I come to sacrifice to Yahweh" (לַיהוָה לִזְבֹּחַ שָׁלוֹם). He avoids the issue by telling what is peaceable about his visit. He knows that what he is there to do is not simply worship God, but to create a revolution as an important statesman. He is there to effect a dynastic change and attempt to bring Israel back to active worship of God, from which it was straying.

It must be noted that this does not mean that his deflection of the question asked by the elders is a lie, or even a violation of what Christ teaches about honesty in Matthew 5:37 (But let your 'Yes' be 'Yes,' and your 'No,' 'No.' For whatever is more than these is from the evil one.). He is avoiding trouble by being vague, but not dishonest. By being honest, he can serve God without hurting human ideas, but the focus is on God and God alone.

Questions to ask:
- Which of the words, lines, or ideas do you recognize from Masonic Work? (Remember to not write them down)
- How do these words, lines, or ideas take the meaning of the degrees and Masonic work and focus them to help make our lives more fit for the Builder's purpose and be Good Men and Masons?
- How do these words, lines, or ideas build our Faith in the Great Architect of the Universe?
- Which of these words, lines, or ideas OTHER than what is used in your Masonic jurisdiction help you to maintain your integrity and work for peace and justice?
- Discuss how these lines could be misunderstood or taken for other purposes that do not glorify God or help you grow as Masons.

1 Samuel 16:1-5

NOTES:

2 Samuel 12:24-25

²⁴Then David comforted his wife Bathsheba, and he went to her and lay with her. So she gave birth to a son, and they named him Solomon. Now the LORD loved the child ²⁵and sent word through Nathan the prophet to name him Jedidiah because the LORD loved him.

    The way that our modern world works, names are legal descriptors of a person. We have one name that is printed on our birth certificates, and only a few times does that change, most commonly due to marriage, confirmation, or birth of a child with the same name. Sometimes in the modern world, we might remember that most of our family names come from an ancestor's occupations (Miller, Smith, Cooper, Fletcher, Baker, etc.), where they were from (deLyon, Von Trapp, etc.), or a characteristic about them (Swartzkopf, Blanche, Whitehead, etc.). In ancient Israel, often people had several names, and people were often called by their function instead of their given name. Solomon was not only Solomon, he was also Jedidiah.

    Jedidiah means *beloved of the LORD*. The term for the "Lord loved him" (בעבור יהוה) at the end of verse 25 in Hebrew means *"for the sake of the LORD."* Solomon was called Jedidiah (meaning *beloved of Yahweh*) by Nathan the prophet, the Chronicler (I Chronicles 22:9) assuming that David was told by Yahweh that his son's name should be Solomon (*peaceful*).

    If we are to hold Solomon as an ideal in some ways (at least in his early days during the building of the Temple), we need to focus on who God told us he was to be: peaceful and beloved of God. To think that his name was just a name is to lose a lot of how Hebrew stories were told. In English, it is often advisable to read *Pilgrim's Progress* by

2 Samuel 12:24-25

Bunyan to see this point made as we can understand it better.

As a note, Bathsheba (or *Bath-shua* in some translations) has two meanings: *Daughter of an Oath* or *Daughter of Seven*. If we interpret it as *Daughter of an Oath*, then the question is what oath had been given to her (marriage to Uriah) or to her father Ammiel/Eliam, a spy for Moses in Numbers 13:12. Since she was the object of several oaths broken by David, it is an important question. If her name is translated as *Daughter of Seven*, then it is a mystical name that refers to God in astonishing ways, as seven is the number of perfection.

Questions to ask:
- Which of the words, lines, or ideas do you recognize from Masonic Work? (Remember to not write them down)
- How do these words, lines, or ideas take the meaning of the degrees and Masonic work and focus them to help make our lives more fit for the Builder's purpose and be Good Men and Masons?
- How do these words, lines, or ideas build our Faith in the Great Architect of the Universe?
- Which of these words, lines, or ideas OTHER than what is used in your Masonic jurisdiction help you to maintain your integrity and work for peace and justice?
- Discuss how these lines could be misunderstood or taken for other purposes that do not glorify God or help you grow as Masons.

NOTES:

2 Samuel 12:24-25

2 Samuel 24:16-25 (NIV)

¹⁶ When the angel stretched out his hand to destroy Jerusalem, the LORD relented concerning the disaster and said to the angel who was afflicting the people, "Enough! Withdraw your hand." The angel of the LORD was then at the threshing floor of Araunah the Jebusite.

¹⁷ When David saw the angel who was striking down the people, he said to the LORD, "I have sinned; I, the shepherd, have done wrong. These are but sheep. What have they done? Let your hand fall on me and my family." ¹⁸ On that day Gad went to David and said to him, "Go up and build an altar to the LORD on the threshing floor of Araunah the Jebusite." ¹⁹ So David went up, as the LORD had commanded through Gad. ²⁰ When Araunah looked and saw the king and his officials coming toward him, he went out and bowed down before the king with his face to the ground. ²¹ Araunah said, "Why has my lord the king come to his servant?" "To buy your threshing floor," David answered, "so I can build an altar to the LORD, that the plague on the people may be stopped." ²² Araunah said to David, "Let my lord the king take whatever he wishes and offer it up. Here are oxen for the burnt offering, and here are threshing sledges and ox yokes for the wood. ²³ Your Majesty, Araunah gives all this to the king." Araunah also said to him, "May the LORD your God accept you." ²⁴ But the king replied to Araunah, "No, I insist on paying you for it. I will not sacrifice to the LORD my God burnt offerings that cost me nothing." So David bought the threshing floor and the oxen and paid fifty shekels of silver for them. ²⁵ David built an altar to the LORD there and sacrificed burnt offerings and fellowship offerings. Then the LORD answered his

2 Samuel 24:16-25 (NIV)
prayer in behalf of the land, and the plague on Israel was stopped.

Most masonic writings leave out the first few verses, instead starting at verse 18, but context is important. Why people do a thing is sometimes more important than what they do. David was trying to lessen the impact of a plague on his people by making a sacrifice in an appropriate place. There was no Temple yet, and the Ark of the Covenant had entered Jerusalem back in 2 Samuel 6, but was not yet in a permanent spot. As with other names, Araunah was also translated as Ornan in different manuscripts.

This passage reminds us all that things given to us should not be offered to God, as they did not cost us anything, so do not mean as much to us. Things we offer are representations of ourselves: our efforts, our skills and abilities, and our values. Should we ever give God nothing? This is where many churches remind people rightly that it is not about writing a check, but about offering yourself, your time and talents, and what resources you have to build the Kingdom of God.

In no manuscripts can be found any references to the shape of the threshing floor. These tended to be organic in shape, or demarked by fences to which could be hung fabric to gather the wheat that was thrashed, in which cases the fences were either round or rectangular.

Questions to ask:
- Which of the words, lines, or ideas do you recognize from Masonic Work? (Remember to not write them down)
- How do these words, lines, or ideas take the meaning of the degrees and Masonic work and focus them to help make our lives more fit for the Builder's purpose and be Good Men and Masons?

2 Samuel 24:16-25 (NIV)
- How do these words, lines, or ideas build our Faith in the Great Architect of the Universe?
- Which of these words, lines, or ideas OTHER than what is used in your Masonic jurisdiction help you to maintain your integrity and work for peace and justice?
- Discuss how these lines could be misunderstood or taken for other purposes that do not glorify God or help you grow as Masons.

NOTES:

1 Kings 5:15-18

¹⁵ And Solomon had threescore and ten thousand that bare burdens, and fourscore thousand hewers in the mountains; ¹⁶ Beside the chief of Solomon's officers which were over the work, three thousand and three hundred, which ruled over the people that wrought in the work. ¹⁷ And the king commanded, and they brought great stones, costly stones, and hewed stones, to lay the foundation of the house. ¹⁸ And Solomon's builders and Hiram's builders did hew them, and the stonesquarers: so they prepared timber and stones to build the house.

Solomon's Temple was one of the most massive building project in the history of the land of Canaan. Seventy thousand laborers and 80,000 lumberjacks supervised by 3300 foremen did a tremendous amount of work in this international building effort that increased the size of Jerusalem's population and required huge resources to feed and house them all.

It should be noted that the carpenters and stonesquarers worked separately, but still together. Dimensions had to be agreed upon and set for all elements of the work to progress in uniformity. From this, the lesson must be learned that the only way to move forward is in unity and humility. No one worker could say he was better or more valuable, and ach had to be appreciated for what he did for the overall plan of the building effort.

Questions to ask:
- Which of the words, lines, or ideas do you recognize from Masonic Work? (Remember to not write them down)

1 Kings 5:15-18

- How do these words, lines, or ideas take the meaning of the degrees and Masonic work and focus them to help make our lives more fit for the Builder's purpose and be Good Men and Masons?
- How do these words, lines, or ideas build our Faith in the Great Architect of the Universe?
- Which of these words, lines, or ideas OTHER than what is used in your Masonic jurisdiction help you to maintain your integrity and work for peace and justice?
- Discuss how these lines could be misunderstood or taken for other purposes that do not glorify God or help you grow as Masons.

NOTES:

1 Kings 6: 1-10

¹In the four hundred and eightieth year after the Israelites had come out of the land of Egypt, in the month of Ziv, the second month of the fourth year of Solomon's reign over Israel, he began to build the house of the LORD. ²The house that King Solomon built for the LORD was sixty cubits long, twenty cubits wide, and thirty cubits high. ³The portico at the front of the main hall of the temple was twenty cubits long, extending across the width of the temple and projecting out ten cubits in front of the temple. ⁴He also had narrow windows framed high in the temple. ⁵Against the walls of the temple and the inner sanctuary, Solomon built a chambered structure all around the temple, in which he constructed the side rooms. ⁶The bottom floor was five cubits wide, the middle floor six cubits, and the third floor seven cubits. He also placed offset ledges all around the outside of the temple, so that nothing would be inserted into its walls. ⁷The temple was constructed using finished stones cut at the quarry, so that no hammer, chisel, or any iron tool was heard in the temple while it was being built. ⁸The entrance to the bottom floor was on the south side of the temple. A stairway led up to the middle level, and from there to the third floor. ⁹So Solomon built the temple and finished it, roofing it with beams and planks of cedar. ¹⁰He built chambers all along the temple, each five cubits high and attached to the temple with beams of cedar.

It is rare for dates to be pointed out so specifically, but there are a number of other references to these dates, and some translations historically have changed the dates to be from the end of the Exodus instead of the beginning, thus 440 years instead of 480. The month *Ziv* is full of

1 Kings 6: 1-10

meaning of luster and beauty, like the beauty of a new flower. This is a special illusion to the purpose of the time. Solomon inherited a lot of resources from his father, and still needed three years of preparation before he could begin to build the Temple, even though this was a fulfillment of the dreams of David and the People. If we compare this to the information provided in 2 Chronicles 3:1-2, we see:

> [1]Then Solomon began to build the house of the LORD at Jerusalem in mount Moriah, where the LORD appeared unto David his father, in the place that David had prepared in the threshing floor of Ornan the Jebusite. [2]And he began to build in the second day of the second month, in the fourth year of his reign.

The information is the same, thus validating well when this took place. Ornan is the last Jebusite mentioned in the Bible. The Jebusites were a people descended from Canaan, who was Ham's fourth son, thus grandson of Noah. Remember that Ornan had tried to give David the threshing floor, but David would not sacrifice on a place that cost him nothing, so he paid a huge amount of money for the site. Read 1 Chronicles 21:14-30 for that story. In construction of the Temple, Ornan may also be brought up again since his name means "Cedar Tree."

The dimensions of the Temple are provided, and assumption is that a sacred cubit was being used (almost 22"), not an ordinary cubit (just over 20"). The exact measurements are not as important as the ratio. Rooms were offset and increasing in size above, indicating that the ascent would bring people closer to God, as in the number seven as well as proximity to heaven.

All of the stones were cut in the quarry, as cutting stone is loud work, and Temples are supposed to be places of prayer and worship, neither of which can be done well with a lot of banging going on. Solomon's quarries are a topic of debate, as to whether they were in the fields outside

1 Kings 6: 1-10

of the city or in a cave in the city itself. If you go to Jerusalem right now, near the Herodian Gate, is the entrance to Zedekiah's Cave, which tour guides will tell you is the same as Solomon's Quarries, but they also say it is only about 2000 years old. Modern archaeologists often place the quarries at Siloam (*Silwan*), the original site of Jerusalem (when founded by the Jebusites as the town of Jebus) that grew upwards on the mount for protection.

The winding staircase went up from the first to second and then from second to third floors. While there is not mention of the number of stairs for each staircase, it is likely that there were specific numbers used for ritualistic purposes.

Questions to ask:
- Which of the words, lines, or ideas do you recognize from Masonic Work? (Remember to not write them down)
- How do these words, lines, or ideas take the meaning of the degrees and Masonic work and focus them to help make our lives more fit for the Builder's purpose and be Good Men and Masons?
- How do these words, lines, or ideas build our Faith in the Great Architect of the Universe?
- Which of these words, lines, or ideas OTHER than what is used in your Masonic jurisdiction help you to maintain your integrity and work for peace and justice?
- Discuss how these lines could be misunderstood or taken for other purposes that do not glorify God or help you grow as Masons.

1 Kings 6: 1-10

NOTES:

1 Kings 7:13-51

¹³ And king Solomon sent and fetched Hiram out of Tyre. ¹⁴ He was a widow's son of the tribe of Naphtali, and his father was a man of Tyre, a worker in brass: and he was filled with wisdom, and understanding, and cunning to work all works in brass. And he came to king Solomon, and wrought all his work. ¹⁵ For he cast two pillars of brass, of eighteen cubits high apiece: and a line of twelve cubits did compass either of them about. ¹⁶ And he made two chapiters of molten brass, to set upon the tops of the pillars: the height of the one chapiter was five cubits, and the height of the other chapiter was five cubits: ¹⁷ And nets of checker work, and wreaths of chain work, for the chapiters which were upon the top of the pillars; seven for the one chapiter, and seven for the other chapiter. ¹⁸ And he made the pillars, and two rows round about upon the one network, to cover the chapiters that were upon the top, with pomegranates: and so did he for the other chapiter. ¹⁹ And the chapiters that were upon the top of the pillars were of lily work in the porch, four cubits. ²⁰ And the chapiters upon the two pillars had pomegranates also above, over against the belly which was by the network: and the pomegranates were two hundred in rows round about upon the other chapiter. ²¹ And he set up the pillars in the porch of the temple: and he set up the right pillar, and called the name thereof Jachin: and he set up the left pillar, and called the name thereof Boaz. ²² And upon the top of the pillars was lily work: so was the work of the pillars finished. ²³ And he made a molten sea, ten cubits from the one brim to the other: it was round all about, and his height was five cubits: and a line of thirty cubits did

1 Kings 7:13-51

compass it round about. ²⁴ And under the brim of it round about there were knops compassing it, ten in a cubit, compassing the sea round about: the knops were cast in two rows, when it was cast. ²⁵ It stood upon twelve oxen, three looking toward the north, and three looking toward the west, and three looking toward the south, and three looking toward the east: and the sea was set above upon them, and all their hinder parts were inward. ²⁶ And it was an hand breadth thick, and the brim thereof was wrought like the brim of a cup, with flowers of lilies: it contained two thousand baths. ²⁷ And he made ten bases of brass; four cubits was the length of one base, and four cubits the breadth thereof, and three cubits the height of it. ²⁸ And the work of the bases was on this manner: they had borders, and the borders were between the ledges: ²⁹ And on the borders that were between the ledges were lions, oxen, and cherubims: and upon the ledges there was a base above: and beneath the lions and oxen were certain additions made of thin work. ³⁰ And every base had four brasen wheels, and plates of brass: and the four corners thereof had undersetters: under the laver were undersetters molten, at the side of every addition. ³¹ And the mouth of it within the chapiter and above was a cubit: but the mouth thereof was round after the work of the base, a cubit and an half: and also upon the mouth of it were gravings with their borders, foursquare, not round. ³² And under the borders were four wheels; and the axletrees of the wheels were joined to the base: and the height of a wheel was a cubit and half a cubit. ³³ And the work of the wheels was like the work of a chariot wheel: their axletrees, and their naves, and their felloes, and their spokes, were all molten. ³⁴ And there were four undersetters to the four corners of one base: and the undersetters were of the very base itself. ³⁵ And in the top of the base was

1 Kings 7:13-51

there a round compass of half a cubit high: and on the top of the base the ledges thereof and the borders thereof were of the same. ³⁶ For on the plates of the ledges thereof, and on the borders thereof, he graved cherubims, lions, and palm trees, according to the proportion of every one, and additions round about. ³⁷ After this manner he made the ten bases: all of them had one casting, one measure, and one size. ³⁸ Then made he ten lavers of brass: one laver contained forty baths: and every laver was four cubits: and upon every one of the ten bases one laver. ³⁹ And he put five bases on the right side of the house, and five on the left side of the house: and he set the sea on the right side of the house eastward over against the south. ⁴⁰ And Hiram made the lavers, and the shovels, and the basons. So Hiram made an end of doing all the work that he made king Solomon for the house of the LORD: ⁴¹ The two pillars, and the two bowls of the chapiters that were on the top of the two pillars; and the two networks, to cover the two bowls of the chapiters which were upon the top of the pillars; ⁴² And four hundred pomegranates for the two networks, even two rows of pomegranates for one network, to cover the two bowls of the chapiters that were upon the pillars; ⁴³ And the ten bases, and ten lavers on the bases; ⁴⁴ And one sea, and twelve oxen under the sea; ⁴⁵ And the pots, and the shovels, and the basons: and all these vessels, which Hiram made to king Solomon for the house of the LORD, were of bright brass. ⁴⁶ In the plain of Jordan did the king cast them, in the clay ground between Succoth and Zarthan. ⁴⁷ And Solomon left all the vessels unweighed, because they were exceeding many: neither was the weight of the brass found out. ⁴⁸ And Solomon made all the vessels that pertained unto the house of the LORD: the altar of gold, and the

1 Kings 7:13-51

table of gold, whereupon the shewbread was, ⁴⁹ And the candlesticks of pure gold, five on the right side, and five on the left, before the oracle, with the flowers, and the lamps, and the tongs of gold, ⁵⁰ And the bowls, and the snuffers, and the basons, and the spoons, and the censers of pure gold; and the hinges of gold, both for the doors of the inner house, the most holy place, and for the doors of the house, to wit, of the temple. ⁵¹ So was ended all the work that king Solomon made for the house of the LORD. And Solomon brought in the things which David his father had dedicated; even the silver, and the gold, and the vessels, did he put among the treasures of the house of the LORD.

New International Version reads verse 41 as: "the two pillars; the two bowl-shaped capitals on top of the pillars; the two sets of network decorating the two bowl-shaped capitals on top of the pillars;" The Hebrew word here, *gullot* (גלת) is also used to describe springs, as in Joshua 15:19 and Judges 1:15. The interpretation of them as "globes" is a translating issue, as globes are made up of two bowls. These bowls, if not strictly for ornamentation as is the consensus thought, are likely to have been used as springs of water for the collection of rain (unlikely), or for burning of oil above the pillars (slightly more likely).

The name Jachin (יכין) means *God will Establish*, and is a future form of כון (kun). Establish here can be seen as not only building, as in laying a foundation, but developing a foundation as in faith or understanding. There are four Jachins in the Bible: A son of Simeon, son of Jacob, who would become the patriarch of the יכיני, the Jachinites in Numbers 26:12 (in 1 Chronicles 4:24 he's called Jarib). The second Jachin was mentioned among the descendants of Aaron (1 Chronicles 24:17). Another Jachin was a priest in the time of Nehemiah (Nehemiah 11:10). Finally, the name

1 Kings 7:13-51

is used for the right pillar in front of Solomon's temple, the left one being named Boaz (1 Kings 7:21).

Questions to ask:
- Which of the words, lines, or ideas do you recognize from Masonic Work? (Remember to not write them down)
- How do these words, lines, or ideas take the meaning of the degrees and Masonic work and focus them to help make our lives more fit for the Builder's purpose and be Good Men and Masons?
- How do these words, lines, or ideas build our Faith in the Great Architect of the Universe?
- Which of these words, lines, or ideas OTHER than what is used in your Masonic jurisdiction help you to maintain your integrity and work for peace and justice?
- Discuss how these lines could be misunderstood or taken for other purposes that do not glorify God or help you grow as Masons.

NOTES:

1 Chronicles 3:1-9

> ¹These were the sons of David who were born to him in Hebron:
>> The firstborn was Amnon, by Ahinoam of Jezreel;
>> the second was Daniel, by Abigail of Carmel;
>> ²the third was Absalom the son of Maacah daughter of King Talmai of Geshur;
>> the fourth was Adonijah the son of Haggith;
>> ³the fifth was Shephatiah by Abital;
>> and the sixth was Ithream by his wife Eglah.
>
> ⁴These six sons were born to David in Hebron, where he reigned seven years and six months. And David reigned in Jerusalem thirty-three years, ⁵and these sons were born to him in Jerusalem:
>> Shimea, Shobab, Nathan, and Solomon. These four were born to him by Bathshebab daughter of Ammiel.
>
> ⁶David's other sons were Ibhar, Elishua, Eliphelet, ⁷Nogah, Nepheg, Japhia, ⁸Elishama, Eliada, and Eliphelet—nine in all. ⁹These were all the sons of David, besides the sons by his concubines. And Tamar was their sister.

When we look at Solomon, we ask why he inherited the crown, since he was not the firstborn, but the tenth-born son. While some authors have tried to point out that Solomon (which means Peace) could be a representation of the tenth plague of Egypt, in which all first-born sons died, this is often overlooked as less than optimal theory. The number ten is represented by the letter *Yod*, which is often important in many Masonic bodies. *Yod* is a letter and a number, but it is also the word "*hand.*" If Solomon was the

1 Chronicles 3:1-9

tenth son, the Kabbalistic[4] person would see peace as the hand of God resting upon Israel and seeing the hand of God to work in building the Temple. Since Solomon was the fourth son of Bathsheba, that means that he was also the legal heir to Uriah the Hittite whom David has slain, this Solomon was able to redeem the family line of Uriah, whose name means the *Light of God*.

Questions to ask:
- Which of the words, lines, or ideas do you recognize from Masonic Work? (Remember to not write them down)
- How do these words, lines, or ideas take the meaning of the degrees and Masonic work and focus them to help make our lives more fit for the Builder's purpose and be Good Men and Masons?
- How do these words, lines, or ideas build our Faith in the Great Architect of the Universe?
- Which of these words, lines, or ideas OTHER than what is used in your Masonic jurisdiction help you to maintain your integrity and work for peace and justice?
- Discuss how these lines could be misunderstood or taken for other purposes that do not glorify God or help you grow as Masons.

NOTES:

---

[4] Someone who puts a lot of significance on numbers and their meaning in esoteric ways.

2 Chronicles 2:1-18

¹And Solomon determined to build an house for the name of the LORD, and an house for his kingdom. ²And Solomon told out threescore and ten thousand men to bear burdens, and fourscore thousand to hew in the mountain, and three thousand and six hundred to oversee them. ³And Solomon sent to Huram the king of Tyre, saying, As thou didst deal with David my father, and didst send him cedars to build him an house to dwell therein, even so deal with me. ⁴Behold, I build an house to the name of the LORD my God, to dedicate it to him, and to burn before him sweet incense, and for the continual shewbread, and for the burnt offerings morning and evening, on the sabbaths, and on the new moons, and on the solemn feasts of the LORD our God. This is an ordinance for ever to Israel. ⁵And the house which I build is great: for great is our God above all gods. ⁶But who is able to build him an house, seeing the heaven and heaven of heavens cannot contain him? who am I then, that I should build him an house, save only to burn sacrifice before him? ⁷Send me now therefore a man cunning to work in gold, and in silver, and in brass, and in iron, and in purple, and crimson, and blue, and that can skill to grave with the cunning men that are with me in Judah and in Jerusalem, whom David my father did provide. ⁸Send me also cedar trees, fir trees, and algum trees, out of Lebanon: for I know that thy servants can skill to cut timber in Lebanon; and, behold, my servants shall be with thy servants, ⁹Even to prepare me timber in abundance: for the house which I am about to build shall be wonderful great. ¹⁰And, behold, I will give to thy servants, the hewers that cut timber, twenty thousand measures

2 Chronicles 2:1-18

of beaten wheat, and twenty thousand measures of barley, and twenty thousand baths of wine, and twenty thousand baths of oil. [11]Then Huram the king of Tyre answered in writing, which he sent to Solomon, Because the LORD hath loved his people, he hath made thee king over them. [12]Huram said moreover, Blessed be the LORD God of Israel, that made heaven and earth, who hath given to David the king a wise son, endued with prudence and understanding, that might build an house for the LORD, and an house for his kingdom. [13]And now I have sent a cunning man, endued with understanding, of Huram my father's, [14]The son of a woman of the daughters of Dan, and his father was a man of Tyre, skillful to work in gold, and in silver, in brass, in iron, in stone, and in timber, in purple, in blue, and in fine linen, and in crimson; also to grave any manner of graving, and to find out every device which shall be put to him, with thy cunning men, and with the cunning men of my lord David thy father. [15]Now therefore the wheat, and the barley, the oil, and the wine, which my lord hath spoken of, let him send unto his servants: [16]And we will cut wood out of Lebanon, as much as thou shalt need: and we will bring it to thee in floats by sea to Joppa; and thou shalt carry it up to Jerusalem. [17]And Solomon numbered all the strangers that were in the land of Israel, after the numbering wherewith David his father had numbered them; and they were found an hundred and fifty thousand and three thousand and six hundred. [18]And he set threescore and ten thousand of them to be bearers of burdens, and fourscore thousand to be hewers in the mountain, and three thousand and six hundred overseers to set the people a work.

2 Chronicles 2:1-18

This section, which has some overlap with 1 Kings 5:1-12, describes in good detail the beginning of the plan for building the Temple. There was a good relationship between Tyre and Israel, and the king of Tyre had supplied building materials and workers to David for the building of his house, the royal palace (see 2 Samuel 5:11, 1 Chronicles 14:1). This was not just a favor or work for free, as Hiram and Solomon made a peace pact (2 Samuel 5:2), and Solomon paid Hiram's men and supplied them food and lodging, and more importantly gave twenty cities in Galilee to Tyre. Upon inspection, Hiram didn't like these towns very much and the area in which they were situated was called **Cabul** (meaning *"what does not please"*) ever since (1 Kings 9:13). This is where it is asked of Hiram was his name or his title in Hebrew, as the name means *"brother,"* and you would need to have a good, brotherly relationship for the disappointing property to not break the contract that the two of them had agreed to for building the Temple. It is worth noting that king Hiram is called Huram (חורם) in Chronicles, and Hirom (חירום, Hirom) in 1 Kings 5. Also note the similarity between these names Hiram (חירם) / Huram (חורם) and the names Horem (חרם) / Harim (חרם) from the verb חרם (*haram*, or *dedicated to God*). The Brown-Driver-Briggs (BDB) Theological Dictionary doesn't translate the name Hiram, but decrees that it is an abbreviated form of the name אחירם (*Ahiram*), and that name consists of the verb רום (*rum*), meaning to be high, and the common noun אח (*ah*), meaning brother. Indeed, Hiram was the highly-thought of brother, perhaps a senior warden, or a Grand Master since he was head of his jurisdiction and the highest of brothers there. There is another word derived from this same form אח (*ah*); the exclamation of grief, as used in Ezekiel 6:11 and 21:15: Ach! Alas! It's similarly unclear where this word comes from, but perhaps its origin is comparable to the mechanism that gave modern English the exclamation "**O brother!**"

2 Chronicles 2:1-18

Since the word Tyre literally means "*rock*" or "*stone*," it was renowned for stone cutters and masons who crafted out of stone. Some people have speculated that their location on the Mediterranean Sea would have helped them learn the art of corbelling (laying stones slightly inset to form angled passageways through walls, and later arches, in which keystones are necessary to hold the arch together once construction piles are removed.

Hiram later gave Solomon some cities, showing great brotherly love. Solomon latter fortified those cities and occupants moved there from Israel (2 Chronicles 8:2). Later, Solomon built his fleet of ships to trade for gold with Ophir, king Hiram sent sailors to man the vessels (1 Kings 9:27, 10:11, 2 Chronicles 8:18). This shows a great brotherly relationship between the two kings and the two countries.

The famous craftsman of Tyre, the "**widow's son**" from the tribe of Naphtali, who king Solomon contracted to create all the bronze items for the temple (1 Kings 7:13). He is mostly called Hiram, but in 1 Kings 7:40 he's called חירום (*Hirom*) and in 2 Chronicles 4 he's known as חורם (*Huram*). 2 Chronicles 4:16 even speaks of Huram-abi. Huram-abi (in the NAS and NIV translations) would be the brother of a father (uncle), but Hebrew word for uncle is דוד (*dohd*), so there must be another form used here, and for specific purposes. The JSP translation says his name should be translated as "***Hiram the Master Craftsman.***"

Questions to ask:
- Which of the words, lines, or ideas do you recognize from Masonic Work? (Remember to not write them down)
- How do these words, lines, or ideas take the meaning of the degrees and Masonic work and

2 Chronicles 2:1-18

> focus them to help make our lives more fit for the Builder's purpose and be Good Men and Masons?

- How do these words, lines, or ideas build our Faith in the Great Architect of the Universe?
- Which of these words, lines, or ideas OTHER than what is used in your Masonic jurisdiction help you to maintain your integrity and work for peace and justice?
- Discuss how these lines could be misunderstood or taken for other purposes that do not glorify God or help you grow as Masons.

NOTES:

2 Chronicles 3:1-17

¹Then Solomon began to build the house of the LORD at Jerusalem in mount Moriah, where the LORD appeared unto David his father, in the place that David had prepared in the threshing floor of Ornan the Jebusite. ²And he began to build in the second day of the second month, in the fourth year of his reign. ³Now these are the things wherein Solomon was instructed for the building of the house of God. The length by cubits after the first measure was threescore cubits, and the breadth twenty cubits. ⁴And the porch that was in the front of the house, the length of it was according to the breadth of the house, twenty cubits, and the height was an hundred and twenty: and he overlaid it within with pure gold. ⁵And the greater house he cieled with fir tree, which he overlaid with fine gold, and set thereon palm trees and chains. ⁶And he garnished the house with precious stones for beauty: and the gold was gold of Parvaim. ⁷He overlaid also the house, the beams, the posts, and the walls thereof, and the doors thereof, with gold; and graved cherubims on the walls. ⁸And he made the most holy house, the length whereof was according to the breadth of the house, twenty cubits, and the breadth thereof twenty cubits: and he overlaid it with fine gold, amounting to six hundred talents. ⁹And the weight of the nails was fifty shekels of gold. And he overlaid the upper chambers with gold. ¹⁰And in the most holy house he made two cherubims of image work, and overlaid them with gold. ¹¹And the wings of the cherubims were twenty cubits long: one wing of the one cherub was five cubits, reaching to the wall of the house: and the other wing was likewise five cubits, reaching to the wing of the other cherub. ¹²And one wing of the

2 Chronicles 3:1-17

other cherub was five cubits, reaching to the wall of the house: and the other wing was five cubits also, joining to the wing of the other cherub. ¹³The wings of these cherubims spread themselves forth twenty cubits: and they stood on their feet, and their faces were inward. ¹⁴And he made the vail of blue, and purple, and crimson, and fine linen, and wrought cherubims thereon. ¹⁵Also he made before the house two pillars of thirty and five cubits high, and the chapiter that was on the top of each of them was five cubits. ¹⁶And he made chains, as in the oracle, and put them on the heads of the pillars; and made an hundred pomegranates, and put them on the chains. ¹⁷And he reared up the pillars before the temple, one on the right hand, and the other on the left; and called the name of that on the right hand Jachin, and the name of that on the left Boaz.

This section reiterates the material found in 1 Kings 6:1-4. Solomon began construction on the second day of the second month in the fourth year of his reign, showing that there was time for planning and careful consideration, not simply stampeding off to build the house of the LORD in Jerusalem on Mount Moriah. The site where Solomon built the Temple is the spot where David worshipped God and lamented his sins against God, the threshing floor of Ornan the Jebusite.

The site had been a threshing floor, where wheat and chaff were separated, so it is appropriate that the Temple is the spot where worshippers and the unclean are separated. Clean and unclean are separated by a veil in many parts that is composed of four colors: blue, purple, red, and white, all with cherubim embroidered into them.

There is a lot of importance given to the pillars at the entrance to the Temple (see also 1 Kings 7:21). They are named to help those who enter in to recognize that these two words, both dealing with faith, are what are needed.

2 Chronicles 3:1-17

Establishing faith and strengthening faith are the two purposes of the Temple to humanity, while worshipping God is the central purpose of humanity.

Questions to ask:

- Which of the words, lines, or ideas do you recognize from Masonic Work? (Remember to not write them down)
- How do these words, lines, or ideas take the meaning of the degrees and Masonic work and focus them to help make our lives more fit for the Builder's purpose and be Good Men and Masons?
- How do these words, lines, or ideas build our Faith in the Great Architect of the Universe?
- Which of these words, lines, or ideas OTHER than what is used in your Masonic jurisdiction help you to maintain your integrity and work for peace and justice?
- Discuss how these lines could be misunderstood or taken for other purposes that do not glorify God or help you grow as Masons.

NOTES:

2 Chronicles 4:11-18

¹¹In addition, Huram made the pots, shovels, and sprinkling bowls. So Huram finished the work that he had undertaken for King Solomon in the house of God: ¹²the two pillars; the two bowl-shaped capitals atop the pillars; the two sets of network covering both bowls of the capitals atop the pillars; ¹³the four hundred pomegranates for the two sets of network (two rows of pomegranates for each network covering both the bowl-shaped capitals atop the pillars); ¹⁴the stands; the basins on the stands; ¹⁵the Sea; the twelve oxen underneath the Sea; ¹⁶and the pots, shovels, meat forks, and all the other articles. All these objects that Huram-abi made for King Solomon for the house of the LORD were of polished bronze. ¹⁷The king had them cast in clay molds in the plain of the Jordan between Succoth and Zeredah. ¹⁸Solomon made all these articles in such great abundance that the weight of the bronze could not be determined.

This section reiterates, from a slightly different perspective, the material presented earlier in 1 Kings 7:13-51. As with other writings in Chronicles, Hiram appears here as *Huram*, but is shown as a specialist in brass work of exceptional artistry. The bowls and the network, also called wreath, around the top of the pillars is ornamentation to make the pillars more beautiful and represent the abundance of God's grace and blessings.

Of special note here that is not discussed in Kings is the brazen altar. This large altar, called the Sea here (הים - *hayyām*), as if it were the Mediterranean, is the large artificial bowl in which fire and sacrificed would be placed. That the bowl-like Sea of the altar was built above oxen supports was a mild rebuke to those who had wandered in the desert and had erected a golden calf to worship. The sacrifices to God

2 Chronicles 4:11-18

include broken and contrite hearts (Psalm 51:17, but also Psalm 34:18, Isaiah 61:1, and Luke 4:18). To remind all people offering sacrifices that their ancestors had broken faith was to help them not make the same mistakes. To see a bull sacrificed on an altar above bulls was also to remind the people that bulls are also creations of the creator, and cannot be gods themselves when they are sacrificed.

The land between Succoth and Zeredah (or Zeredathah) was full of clay deposits, and had (at that time) sufficient trees to make charcoal to melt bronze and brass. The clay molds, הָאֲדָמָה (*ha'adāmāh*), which are strangely inverted reminders of God creating The Man – *ha'adam* - הָאָדָם – were almost certainly carved in homage to the way that God knelt in the dirt and formed man in Genesis 1:27 and 2:7. God made and blessed us, so Solomon wanted to make and bless things to God's glory and make sure that God got the glory, not the things being made.

Questions to ask:

- Which of the words, lines, or ideas do you recognize from Masonic Work? (Remember to not write them down)
- How do these words, lines, or ideas take the meaning of the degrees and Masonic work and focus them to help make our lives more fit for the Builder's purpose and be Good Men and Masons?
- How do these words, lines, or ideas build our Faith in the Great Architect of the Universe?
- Which of these words, lines, or ideas OTHER than what is used in your Masonic jurisdiction help you to maintain your integrity and work for peace and justice?

2 Chronicles 4:11-18
- Discuss how these lines could be misunderstood or taken for other purposes that do not glorify God or help you grow as Masons.

NOTES:

2 Chronicles 6:12-42

Solomon's Prayer of Dedication

[12]Then Solomon stood before the altar of the LORD in front of the whole assembly of Israel and spread out his hands. [13]Now Solomon had made a bronze platform five cubits long, five cubits wide, and three cubits high,[5] and had placed it in the middle of the courtyard. He stood on it, knelt down before the whole assembly of Israel, spread out his hands toward heaven, [14]and said:

> "O LORD, God of Israel, there is no God like You in heaven or on earth, keeping Your covenant of loving devotion with Your servants who walk before You with all their hearts. [15]You have kept Your promise to Your servant, my father David. What You spoke with Your mouth You have fulfilled with Your hand this day.
>
> [16]Therefore now, O LORD, God of Israel, keep for Your servant, my father David, what You promised when You said: 'You will never fail to have a man to sit before Me on the throne of Israel, if only your descendants guard their way to walk in My Law as you have walked before Me.' [17]And now, O LORD, God of Israel, please confirm what You promised to Your servant David. [18]But will God indeed dwell with man upon the earth? Even heaven, the highest heaven, cannot contain You, much less this temple I have built. [19]Yet regard the prayer and plea of Your servant, O LORD my God, so that You may hear the cry and

---

[5] That is, about 7.5 feet in length and width, and 4.5 feet high (2.3 meters in length and width, and 1.4 meters high)

2 Chronicles 6:12-42

the prayer that Your servant is praying before You. [20]May Your eyes be open toward this temple day and night, toward the place of which You said You would put Your Name there, so that You may hear the prayer that Your servant prays toward this place.[21]Hear the plea of Your servant and Your people Israel when they pray toward this place. May You hear from heaven, Your dwelling place. May You hear and forgive. [22]When a man sins against his neighbor and is required to take an oath, and he comes to take an oath before Your altar in this temple, [23]may You hear from heaven and act. May You judge Your servants, condemning the wicked man by bringing down on his own head what he has done, and justifying the righteous man by rewarding him according to his righteousness. [24]When Your people Israel are defeated before an enemy because they have sinned against You, and they return to You and confess Your name, praying and pleading before You in this house, [25]may You hear from heaven and forgive the sin of Your people Israel. May You restore them to the land You gave to them and their fathers. [26]When the skies are shut and there is no rain because Your people have sinned against You, and they pray toward this place and confess Your name, and they turn from their sins because You have afflicted them, [27]may You hear from heaven and forgive the sin of Your servants, Your people Israel, so that You may teach them the good way in which they should walk. May You send rain on the land that You gave Your people as an inheritance. [28]When famine or pestilence

2 Chronicles 6:12-42

comes upon the land, or blight or mildew or locusts or grasshoppers, when their enemies besiege them in their cities, whatever plague or sickness there is, [29]may whatever prayer or petition Your people Israel make—each knowing his own afflictions and spreading out his hands toward this house— [30]be heard by You from heaven, Your dwelling place. And may You forgive and repay each man according to all his ways, since You know his heart—for You alone know the hearts of men— [31]so that they may fear You and walk in Your ways all the days they live in the land You gave to our fathers. [32]And as for the foreigner who is not of Your people Israel but has come from a distant land because of Your great name and Your mighty hand and outstretched arm—when he comes and prays toward this house, [33]may You hear from heaven, Your dwelling place, and do according to all for which the foreigner calls to You. Then all the peoples of the earth will know Your name and fear You, as do Your people Israel, and they will know that this house I have built is called by Your Name. [34]When Your people go to war against their enemies, wherever You send them, and when they pray to You in the direction of the city You have chosen and the house I have built for Your Name, [35]may You hear from heaven their prayer and their plea, and may You uphold their cause. [36]When they sin against You—for there is no one who does not sin—and You become angry with them and deliver them to an enemy who takes them as captives to a land far or near, [37]and when they come to their

2 Chronicles 6:12-42

senses in the land to which they were taken, and they repent and plead with You in the land of their captors, saying, 'We have sinned and done wrong; we have acted wickedly,' [38]and when they return to You with all their heart and soul in the land of the enemies who took them captive, and when they pray in the direction of the land that You gave to their fathers, the city You have chosen, and the house I have built for Your Name, [39]may You hear in from heaven, Your dwelling place, their prayer and petition, and may You uphold their cause. May You forgive Your people who sinned against You. [40]Now, my God, please may Your eyes be open and Your ears attentive to the prayer offered in this place. [41]Now therefore, arise, O LORD God, and enter Your resting place, You and the ark of Your might. May Your priests, O LORD God, be clothed with salvation, and may Your godly ones rejoice in goodness. [42]O LORD God, do not reject Your anointed one. Remember Your loving devotion to Your servant David."

In this section Solomon's prayer at the dedication of the Temple asks for repentance and forgiveness for all that the Lord has seen wrong with Israel. The idea of the Temple is to bring the understanding and memory of God closer to His people. The Temple was also supposed to be a representation of humanity, in which God dwells because of placing His Image on us. Sections of this prayer are repeated by many more people than only Masons, yet for the same reason: reminding us of our duty to honor God and worship Him with all of our lives. The thick cloud is

2 Chronicles 6:12-42

considered a *theophany*, which is a time that God shows us the He is present with us to give assurance.

Some people have also interpreted the reminder about oaths here to be an admonition that any oath that we take is before God and we must answer to Him for any deviations for those oaths. As discussed earlier, oaths are a natural aspect of life, and God Himself takes oaths that He can bind unto Himself, where we cannot bind ourselves to ourselves, only to Him.

Questions to ask:
- Which of the words, lines, or ideas do you recognize from Masonic Work? (Remember to not write them down)
- How do these words, lines, or ideas take the meaning of the degrees and Masonic work and focus them to help make our lives more fit for the Builder's purpose and be Good Men and Masons?
- How do these words, lines, or ideas build our Faith in the Great Architect of the Universe?
- Which of these words, lines, or ideas OTHER than what is used in your Masonic jurisdiction help you to maintain your integrity and work for peace and justice?
- Discuss how these lines could be misunderstood or taken for other purposes that do not glorify God or help you grow as Masons.

2 Chronicles 6:12-42

NOTES:

2 Chronicles 9:13-28

[13]The weight of gold that came to Solomon each year was 666 talents, [14]not including the revenue from the merchants and traders. And all the Arabian kings and governors of the land also brought gold and silver to Solomon. [15]King Solomon made two hundred large shields of hammered gold; six hundred shekels of hammered gold went into each shield. [16]He also made three hundred small shields of hammered gold; three hundred shekels of gold went into each shield. And the king put them in the House of the Forest of Lebanon.

[17]Additionally, the king made a great throne of ivory and overlaid it with pure gold. [18]The throne had six steps, and a footstool of gold was attached to it. There were armrests on both sides of the seat, with a lion standing beside each armrest. [19]Twelve lions stood on the six steps, one at either end of each step. Nothing like this had ever been made for any kingdom.

[20]All of King Solomon's drinking cups were gold, and all the utensils of the House of the Forest of Lebanon were pure gold. There was no silver, because it was accounted as nothing in the days of Solomon. [21]For the king had the ships of Tarshish that went with Hiram's servants, and once every three years the ships of Tarshish would arrive bearing gold, silver, ivory, apes, and peacocks. [22]So King Solomon surpassed all the kings of the earth in riches and wisdom. [23]All the kings of the earth sought an audience with Solomon to hear the wisdom that God had put in his heart. [24]Year after year, each visitor would bring his tribute: articles of silver and gold, clothing, weapons, spices, horses, and mules. [25]Solomon had 4,000 stalls for horses and chariots, and 12,000 horses, which he stationed

2 Chronicles 9:13-28

in the chariot cities and also with him in Jerusalem. [26]He reigned over all the kings from the Euphrates to the land of the Philistines, as far as the border of Egypt. [27]The king made silver as common in Jerusalem as stones, and cedar as abundant as sycamore in the foothills. [28]Solomon's horses were imported from Egypt and from all the lands.

The first thing that many people notice is that there was 666 talents of Gold. To modern readers there might be a similarity with the "number of the Beast" in Revelation 13:18. This might be a great over-reach, however, on two accounts. First, international exchanges like this were often counted on Assyrian systems of numbers, which was based on six, not ten as is modern numerology. Second, to the ancient Hebrew people, six was a number of insufficiency, not necessarily of evil. Seven was considered a number of Perfection, so six was just short of perfection. Since Satan had been an archangel before his fall, the number six eventually became related to him as having been close to perfection but falling short.

This passage is in concord with 1 Kings 10:14-29, as many of these sections tell the same story from different perspectives to help us understand the fullness of God's message and His plan for us. Solomon had become so famous because of his wisdom that even other monarchs from distant countries came to see for themselves

Note that even silver was thought to be nothing, as there was so much wealth that only gold and gems were given account. Wealth and wonder are not the same as blessings and wisdom. Wisdom and happiness are almost always tied together in scripture, but wealth is often seen as a burden of the soul, and here it is the last thing discussed before Solomon's death. Psalm 19 had stated that fear of the Lord and desire to follow His commandments was more desirable than gold, even much fine gold. Solomon is shown to have had a lot of gold, and all of that wealth will be

2 Chronicles 9:13-28

inherited by a son whom Solomon thought to be incompetent and a terrible person.

Questions to ask:
- Which of the words, lines, or ideas do you recognize from Masonic Work? (Remember to not write them down)
- How do these words, lines, or ideas take the meaning of the degrees and Masonic work and focus them to help make our lives more fit for the Builder's purpose and be Good Men and Masons?
- How do these words, lines, or ideas build our Faith in the Great Architect of the Universe?
- Which of these words, lines, or ideas OTHER than what is used in your Masonic jurisdiction help you to maintain your integrity and work for peace and justice?
- Discuss how these lines could be misunderstood or taken for other purposes that do not glorify God or help you grow as Masons.

NOTES:

2 Chronicles 36:1-23

¹Then the people of the land took Jehoahaz the son of Josiah, and made him king in his father's stead in Jerusalem. ² Jehoahaz was twenty and three years old when he began to reign, and he reigned three months in Jerusalem. ³ And the king of Egypt put him down at Jerusalem, and condemned the land in an hundred talents of silver and a talent of gold. ⁴ And the king of Egypt made Eliakim his brother king over Judah and Jerusalem, and turned his name to Jehoiakim. And Necho took Jehoahaz his brother, and carried him to Egypt. ⁵ Jehoiakim was twenty and five years old when he began to reign, and he reigned eleven years in Jerusalem: and he did that which was evil in the sight of the Lord his God. ⁶ Against him came up Nebuchadnezzar king of Babylon, and bound him in fetters, to carry him to Babylon. ⁷ Nebuchadnezzar also carried of the vessels of the house of the Lord to Babylon, and put them in his temple at Babylon. ⁸ Now the rest of the acts of Jehoiakim, and his abominations which he did, and that which was found in him, behold, they are written in the book of the kings of Israel and Judah: and Jehoiachin his son reigned in his stead. ⁹ Jehoiachin was eight years old when he began to reign, and he reigned three months and ten days in Jerusalem: and he did that which was evil in the sight of the Lord. ¹⁰ And when the year was expired, king Nebuchadnezzar sent, and brought him to Babylon, with the goodly vessels of the house of the Lord, and made Zedekiah his brother king over Judah and Jerusalem. ¹¹ Zedekiah was one and twenty years old when he began to reign, and reigned eleven years in Jerusalem. ¹² And he did that

2 Chronicles 36:1-23

which was evil in the sight of the Lord his God, and humbled not himself before Jeremiah the prophet speaking from the mouth of the Lord. [13] And he also rebelled against king Nebuchadnezzar, who had made him swear by God: but he stiffened his neck, and hardened his heart from turning unto the Lord God of Israel. [14] Moreover all the chief of the priests, and the people, transgressed very much after all the abominations of the heathen; and polluted the house of the Lord which he had hallowed in Jerusalem. [15] And the Lord God of their fathers sent to them by his messengers, rising up betimes, and sending; because he had compassion on his people, and on his dwelling place: [16] But they mocked the messengers of God, and despised his words, and misused his prophets, until the wrath of the Lord arose against his people, till there was no remedy. [17] Therefore he brought upon them the king of the Chaldees, who slew their young men with the sword in the house of their sanctuary, and had no compassion upon young man or maiden, old man, or him that stooped for age: he gave them all into his hand. [18] And all the vessels of the house of God, great and small, and the treasures of the house of the Lord, and the treasures of the king, and of his princes; all these he brought to Babylon. [19] And they burnt the house of God, and brake down the wall of Jerusalem, and burnt all the palaces thereof with fire, and destroyed all the goodly vessels thereof. [20] And them that had escaped from the sword carried he away to Babylon; where they were servants to him and his sons until the reign of the kingdom of Persia: [21] To fulfil the word of the Lord by the mouth of Jeremiah, until the land had enjoyed her sabbaths: for as long as she lay desolate she kept sabbath, to fulfil threescore and ten years. [22] Now in the first year of Cyrus king of Persia, that the word

2 Chronicles 36:1-23

of the Lord spoken by the mouth of Jeremiah might be accomplished, the Lord stirred up the spirit of Cyrus king of Persia, that he made a proclamation throughout all his kingdom, and put it also in writing, saying, [23] Thus saith Cyrus king of Persia, All the kingdoms of the earth hath the Lord God of heaven given me; and he hath charged me to build him an house in Jerusalem, which is in Judah. Who is there among you of all his people? The Lord his God be with him, and let him go up.

This area of Chronicles, and its counter-part in Kings, describes the difficulties of having bad kings who do not follow God's Law. God is amazingly patient, but expects people to be held to account for what they promise to do. Remember that each king had to be enthroned in a ceremony where they were supposed to pledge to defend the Nation and keep it holy.

Jehoahaz was not a king for very long, but as his name means, was one whom *"God had taken a hold of."* Eliakim (*"whom God sets up"*) has his name changed to Jehoiakim: *"God will raise up."* Zedekiah is another of the bad kings described here, and he was bound to Babylon as a vassal king, but rebelled and tried to form an alliance with Egypt. In God's sense of humor, Zedekiah's name reminds us of his fate, as *"God is Righteous."* Jehoiakim is also mentioned as the king who burned scrolls of prophecy in Jeremiah 36:27-32, which is worth reading in reference here.

God ensured His righteousness by dealing justly with these bad kings and seeing that they were punished, yet even then, God was merciful. While the king suffered, it was justice for what he had done to Israel, and while the king's heirs were killed, the Children of Israel were spared. They had rebelled, and were punished, but given hope that they would return home and continue to be blessed. It is a difficult thing to see justice in the bad times, but the Babylonian captivity yielded many good results in people

2 Chronicles 36:1-23

coming to holiness and remembering to thank God for the many blessings that we ignore every day.

Questions to ask:

- Which of the words, lines, or ideas do you recognize from Masonic Work? (Remember to not write them down)
- How do these words, lines, or ideas take the meaning of the degrees and Masonic work and focus them to help make our lives more fit for the Builder's purpose and be Good Men and Masons?
- How do these words, lines, or ideas build our Faith in the Great Architect of the Universe?
- Which of these words, lines, or ideas OTHER than what is used in your Masonic jurisdiction help you to maintain your integrity and work for peace and justice?
- Discuss how these lines could be misunderstood or taken for other purposes that do not glorify God or help you grow as Masons.

NOTES:

Ezra 1:1-11

¹ Now in the first year of Cyrus king of Persia, that the word of the Lord by the mouth of Jeremiah might be fulfilled, the Lord stirred up the spirit of Cyrus king of Persia, that he made a proclamation throughout all his kingdom, and put it also in writing, saying, ² Thus saith Cyrus king of Persia, The Lord God of heaven hath given me all the kingdoms of the earth; and he hath charged me to build him an house at Jerusalem, which is in Judah. ³ Who is there among you of all his people? his God be with him, and let him go up to Jerusalem, which is in Judah, and build the house of the Lord God of Israel, (he is the God,) which is in Jerusalem. ⁴ And whosoever remaineth in any place where he sojourneth, let the men of his place help him with silver, and with gold, and with goods, and with beasts, beside the freewill offering for the house of God that is in Jerusalem. ⁵ Then rose up the chief of the fathers of Judah and Benjamin, and the priests, and the Levites, with all them whose spirit God had raised, to go up to build the house of the Lord which is in Jerusalem. ⁶ And all they that were about them strengthened their hands with vessels of silver, with gold, with goods, and with beasts, and with precious things, beside all that was willingly offered. ⁷ Also Cyrus the king brought forth the vessels of the house of the Lord, which Nebuchadnezzar had brought forth out of Jerusalem, and had put them in the house of his gods; ⁸ Even those did Cyrus king of Persia bring forth by the hand of Mithredath the treasurer, and numbered them unto Sheshbazzar, the prince of Judah. ⁹ And this is the number of them: thirty chargers of gold, a thousand chargers of silver, nine and twenty knives, ¹⁰ Thirty basons of

Ezra 1:1-11

gold, silver basons of a second sort four hundred and ten, and other vessels a thousand. [11] All the vessels of gold and of silver were five thousand and four hundred. All these did Sheshbazzar bring up with them of the captivity that were brought up from Babylon unto Jerusalem.

Cyrus was a king of Persia, but was not outside of the influence of God. God placed upon Cyrus' heart the desire to do good and restore the Temple. The Second Temple was not as beautiful as the First had been, but it was an opportunity for the Children of Israel to look past beauty of a façade to the beauty of the heart that worships God. When the Israelites departed Persia, some did not want to go, as their lives had been in Persia for so long. Most had never known Jerusalem. Most even had Persian names, like Sheshbazzar, whose name means something like *"worshipper of fire"* in Persian, but in Hebrew it becomes something like *"one who purifies at a forge."*

For Masons, it is an important lesson that Sheshbazzar led the first wave of the Jews back to Jerusalem before Zerubbabel, Jeshua, Nehemiah, and Ezra made their historic return. Sheshbazzar had the money, but to reestablish the city, not rebuild the Temple and the walls. The foundations have to be set before the structure is finalized, and Sheshbazzar was set to establish the city again.

Questions to ask:
- Which of the words, lines, or ideas do you recognize from Masonic Work? (Remember to not write them down)
- How do these words, lines, or ideas take the meaning of the degrees and Masonic work and

Ezra 1:1-11
> focus them to help make our lives more fit for the Builder's purpose and be Good Men and Masons?
- How do these words, lines, or ideas build our Faith in the Great Architect of the Universe?
- Which of these words, lines, or ideas OTHER than what is used in your Masonic jurisdiction help you to maintain your integrity and work for peace and justice?
- Discuss how these lines could be misunderstood or taken for other purposes that do not glorify God or help you grow as Masons.

NOTES:

Ezra 3:1-13

¹And when the seventh month was come, and the children of Israel were in the cities, the people gathered themselves together as one man to Jerusalem. ² Then stood up Jeshua the son of Jozadak, and his brethren the priests, and Zerubbabel the son of Shealtiel, and his brethren, and builded the altar of the God of Israel, to offer burnt offerings thereon, as it is written in the law of Moses the man of God. ³ And they set the altar upon his bases; for fear was upon them because of the people of those countries: and they offered burnt offerings thereon unto the LORD, even burnt offerings morning and evening. ⁴ They kept also the feast of tabernacles, as it is written, and offered the daily burnt offerings by number, according to the custom, as the duty of every day required; ⁵ And afterward offered the continual burnt offering, both of the new moons, and of all the set feasts of the LORD that were consecrated, and of every one that willingly offered a freewill offering unto the LORD. ⁶ From the first day of the seventh month began they to offer burnt offerings unto the LORD. But the foundation of the temple of the LORD was not yet laid. ⁷ They gave money also unto the masons, and to the carpenters; and meat, and drink, and oil, unto them of Zidon, and to them of Tyre, to bring cedar trees from Lebanon to the sea of Joppa, according to the grant that they had of Cyrus king of Persia. ⁸ Now in the second year of their coming unto the house of God at Jerusalem, in the second month, began Zerubbabel the son of Shealtiel, and Jeshua the son of Jozadak, and the remnant of their brethren the priests and the Levites, and all they that

Ezra 3:1-13

were come out of the captivity unto Jerusalem; and appointed the Levites, from twenty years old and upward, to set forward the work of the house of the LORD. [9] Then stood Jeshua with his sons and his brethren, Kadmiel and his sons, the sons of Judah, together, to set forward the workmen in the house of God: the sons of Henadad, with their sons and their brethren the Levites. [10] And when the builders laid the foundation of the temple of the LORD, they set the priests in their apparel with trumpets, and the Levites the sons of Asaph with cymbals, to praise the LORD, after the ordinance of David king of Israel. [11] And they sang together by course in praising and giving thanks unto the LORD; because he is good, for his mercy endureth for ever toward Israel. And all the people shouted with a great shout, when they praised the LORD, because the foundation of the house of the LORD was laid. [12] But many of the priests and Levites and chief of the fathers, who were ancient men, that had seen the first house, when the foundation of this house was laid before their eyes, wept with a loud voice; and many shouted aloud for joy: [13] So that the people could not discern the noise of the shout of joy from the noise of the weeping of the people: for the people shouted with a loud shout, and the noise was heard afar off.

This is a moment when God's promises were being fulfilled and He waited for the response of His people. This group of men returned as they were supposed to, ready to rebuild the temple, and consecrated the land where the Temple would be rebuilt to honor God. There was no simple offering, but they kept offering thanks to God throughout the day. They knew that it had not been kept well, and may even have been desecrated by pagans, so the cleaning was important. They made sure to abide by the

Ezra 3:1-13

rules of worship and did not neglect the festival of tabernacles that was so important during the exile.

The names of these people are important here, especially remember that they are named while in captivity in Persia. Shealtiel means "*I have asked God*" while Jozadak means "*God has made Just.*" Henadad means "*favor of the Beloved.*" Kadmiel is a tough name to translate, as it can mean several things, from "*God is Ancient*" to "*God is Rising*" or "*God is in the East.*" Ancient, rising, and in the east are important to us as we now use the term orientation to mean set on a path instead of the literal meaning of facing someone East towards the rising sun, the eternal way of finding our way. Remember that maps used to all have the east at the top of the map so that each morning you could rise, align the map with the sun, and you knew where you were as you were then (literally) oriented- facing the rising sun in the east. All of the names refer to the return to Jerusalem as a homecoming and as a restoration, as Jeshua, whose name is the same as Joshua and Jesus, meaning "*Salvation.*"

Questions to ask:
- Which of the words, lines, or ideas do you recognize from Masonic Work? (Remember to not write them down)
- How do these words, lines, or ideas take the meaning of the degrees and Masonic work and focus them to help make our lives more fit for the Builder's purpose and be Good Men and Masons?
- How do these words, lines, or ideas build our Faith in the Great Architect of the Universe?
- Which of these words, lines, or ideas OTHER than what is used in your Masonic jurisdiction help you to maintain your integrity and work for peace and justice?

Ezra 3:1-13
- Discuss how these lines could be misunderstood or taken for other purposes that do not glorify God or help you grow as Masons.

NOTES:

Ezra 4:1-24

^{1}Now when the adversaries of Judah and Benjamin heard that the children of the captivity builded the temple unto the LORD God of Israel; ^{2}Then they came to Zerubbabel, and to the chief of the fathers, and said unto them, Let us build with you: for we seek your God, as ye do; and we do sacrifice unto him since the days of Esarhaddon king of Assur, which brought us up hither. ^{3}But Zerubbabel, and Jeshua, and the rest of the chief of the fathers of Israel, said unto them, Ye have nothing to do with us to build an house unto our God; but we ourselves together will build unto the LORD God of Israel, as king Cyrus the king of Persia hath commanded us. ^{4}Then the people of the land weakened the hands of the people of Judah, and troubled them in building, ^{5}And hired counsellors against them, to frustrate their purpose, all the days of Cyrus king of Persia, even until the reign of Darius king of Persia. ^{6}And in the reign of Ahasuerus, in the beginning of his reign, wrote they unto him an accusation against the inhabitants of Judah and Jerusalem. ^{7}And in the days of Artaxerxes wrote Bishlam, Mithredath, Tabeel, and the rest of their companions, unto Artaxerxes king of Persia; and the writing of the letter was written in the Syrian tongue, and interpreted in the Syrian tongue. ^{8}Rehum the chancellor and Shimshai the scribe wrote a letter against Jerusalem to Artaxerxes the king in this sort: ^{9}Then wrote Rehum the chancellor, and Shimshai the scribe, and the rest of their companions; the Dinaites, the Apharsathchites, the Tarpelites, the Apharsites, the Archevites, the Babylonians, the Susanchites, the Dehavites, and the Elamites, ^{10}And the rest of the nations whom the great and noble Asnapper brought over, and set in

Ezra 4:1-24

the cities of Samaria, and the rest that are on this side the river, and at such a time. ¹¹This is the copy of the letter that they sent unto him, even unto Artaxerxes the king; Thy servants the men on this side the river, and at such a time. ¹²Be it known unto the king, that the Jews which came up from thee to us are come unto Jerusalem, building the rebellious and the bad city, and have set up the walls thereof, and joined the foundations. ¹³Be it known now unto the king, that, if this city be builded, and the walls set up again, then will they not pay toll, tribute, and custom, and so thou shalt endamage the revenue of the kings. ¹⁴Now because we have maintenance from the king's palace, and it was not meet for us to see the king's dishonour, therefore have we sent and certified the king; ¹⁵That search may be made in the book of the records of thy fathers: so shalt thou find in the book of the records, and know that this city is a rebellious city, and hurtful unto kings and provinces, and that they have moved sedition within the same of old time: for which cause was this city destroyed. ¹⁶We certify the king that, if this city be builded again, and the walls thereof set up, by this means thou shalt have no portion on this side the river. ¹⁷Then sent the king an answer unto Rehum the chancellor, and to Shimshai the scribe, and to the rest of their companions that dwell in Samaria, and unto the rest beyond the river, Peace, and at such a time. ¹⁸The letter which ye sent unto us hath been plainly read before me. ¹⁹And I commanded, and search hath been made, and it is found that this city of old time hath made insurrection against kings, and that rebellion and sedition have been made therein. ²⁰There have been mighty kings also over Jerusalem, which have ruled over all countries beyond the river; and toll, tribute, and custom, was paid unto them. ²¹Give ye now commandment to cause these men to cease, and that this city be not

Ezra 4:1-24

builded, until another commandment shall be given from me. [22] Take heed now that ye fail not to do this: why should damage grow to the hurt of the kings? [23] Now when the copy of king Artaxerxes' letter was read before Rehum, and Shimshai the scribe, and their companions, they went up in haste to Jerusalem unto the Jews, and made them to cease by force and power. [24] Then ceased the work of the house of God which is at Jerusalem. So it ceased unto the second year of the reign of Darius king of Persia.

    No matter where you are, or when in history you are, those who seek to serve God will find opposition from those who seek to serve only themselves. In verse 5 we see that lawyers were even hired to impede the construction work. The letter that they send relies on bigotry and the past, instead of seeing the people that the king had sent as being the faithful remnant whom God wanted to be there.

    It is worth taking a moment to discuss names again here. Bishlam as a name is supposed to mean *"in Peace,"* but can mean *"son of silence."* Mithredath means *"dedicated to Mithra."* Mithra was one of the most violent of the military Gods, and one whom Freemasons are almost always explicitly taught to oppose. Tabeel's name is often mistranslated as *"God is Good"* instead of the actual meaning of *"Good for nothing."* All of these persons conspired to keep the Jews from rebuilding the city walls and the Temple during the time of Artaxerxes. History here repeats itself with Rehum and Shimshai repeating this correspondence with the emperor to hold fast to their power.

    In the names, there is a bit of a joke here, as Rehum and Shimshai mean *"compassionate"* and *"sunny"* respectively. They are far from showing compassion while raining on the Israelite parade. The lessons of integrity and truth are represented here well, however, since God will not allow

Ezra 4:1-24

falsehood to override His will for long. The minor victories of evil are always lost to the greater victories of God.

Questions to ask:
- Which of the words, lines, or ideas do you recognize from Masonic Work? (Remember to not write them down)
- How do these words, lines, or ideas take the meaning of the degrees and Masonic work and focus them to help make our lives more fit for the Builder's purpose and be Good Men and Masons?
- How do these words, lines, or ideas build our Faith in the Great Architect of the Universe?
- Which of these words, lines, or ideas OTHER than what is used in your Masonic jurisdiction help you to maintain your integrity and work for peace and justice?
- Discuss how these lines could be misunderstood or taken for other purposes that do not glorify God or help you grow as Masons.

NOTES:

Ezra 5:1-17

Then the prophets, Haggai the prophet, and Zechariah the son of Iddo, prophesied unto the Jews that were in Judah and Jerusalem in the name of the God of Israel, even unto them. ²Then rose up Zerubbabel the son of Shealtiel, and Jeshua the son of Jozadak, and began to build the house of God which is at Jerusalem: and with them were the prophets of God helping them. ³At the same time came to them Tatnai, governor on this side the river, and Shetharboznai and their companions, and said thus unto them, Who hath commanded you to build this house, and to make up this wall? ⁴Then said we unto them after this manner, What are the names of the men that make this building? ⁵But the eye of their God was upon the elders of the Jews, that they could not cause them to cease, till the matter came to Darius: and then they returned answer by letter concerning this matter. ⁶The copy of the letter that Tatnai, governor on this side the river, and Shetharboznai and his companions the Apharsachites, which were on this side the river, sent unto Darius the king: ⁷They sent a letter unto him, wherein was written thus; Unto Darius the king, all peace. ⁸Be it known unto the king, that we went into the province of Judea, to the house of the great God, which is builded with great stones, and timber is laid in the walls, and this work goeth fast on, and prospereth in their hands. ⁹Then asked we those elders, and said unto them thus, Who commanded you to build this house, and to make up these walls? ¹⁰We asked their names also, to certify thee, that we might write the names of the men that were the chief of them. ¹¹And thus they returned us answer, saying, We are the servants of the God of heaven and earth, and build the house

Ezra 5:1-17

that was builded these many years ago, which a great king of Israel builded and set up. [12] But after that our fathers had provoked the God of heaven unto wrath, he gave them into the hand of Nebuchadnezzar the king of Babylon, the Chaldean, who destroyed this house, and carried the people away into Babylon. [13] But in the first year of Cyrus the king of Babylon the same king Cyrus made a decree to build this house of God. [14] And the vessels also of gold and silver of the house of God, which Nebuchadnezzar took out of the temple that was in Jerusalem, and brought them into the temple of Babylon, those did Cyrus the king take out of the temple of Babylon, and they were delivered unto one, whose name was Sheshbazzar, whom he had made governor; [15] And said unto him, Take these vessels, go, carry them into the temple that is in Jerusalem, and let the house of God be builded in his place. [16] Then came the same Sheshbazzar, and laid the foundation of the house of God which is in Jerusalem: and since that time even until now hath it been in building, and yet it is not finished. [17] Now therefore, if it seem good to the king, let there be search made in the king's treasure house, which is there at Babylon, whether it be so, that a decree was made of Cyrus the king to build this house of God at Jerusalem, and let the king send his pleasure to us concerning this matter.

Tatnai (whose name amusingly means *"a gift"*), was a satrap (provincial governor) of the province west of the Euphrates in the time of Darius Hystaspes (Ezra 5:3,6; 6:6,13). He and his colleague Shetharboznai (whose name is Persian for *"star of splendor"*), who was a Persian officer of rank in the reign of Darius, tried to limit the rebuilding of the Temple and the city walls. They knew that if the Temple was rebuilt, it would take away from their power and the

Ezra 5:1-17

amount of money that they made from that region as it gained autonomy. They sent a message to Darius, hoping that it would reinforce their position, but instead it opened up the histories and brought to light the original tale of Sheshbazzar from Ezra 1. By trying to limit the work, Tatnai and Shetharboznai wound up being instruments of God's Will and helping advance the rebuilding.

This lesson serves to remind us all to seek truth and focus on our work, not try to limit other people whom we know to be doing good. Seeking to protect power is almost always a desperate admission that we are insecure of our own power and authority. Humility is supposed to be an overwhelming attribute of Masons, especially when in the service of the Most High God.

Questions to ask:
- Which of the words, lines, or ideas do you recognize from Masonic Work? (Remember to not write them down)
- How do these words, lines, or ideas take the meaning of the degrees and Masonic work and focus them to help make our lives more fit for the Builder's purpose and be Good Men and Masons?
- How do these words, lines, or ideas build our Faith in the Great Architect of the Universe?
- Which of these words, lines, or ideas OTHER than what is used in your Masonic jurisdiction help you to maintain your integrity and work for peace and justice?
- Discuss how these lines could be misunderstood or taken for other purposes that do not glorify God or help you grow as Masons.

Ezra 5:1-17

NOTES:

Psalm 22

¹My God, my God, why have You forsaken me?
    Why are You so far from saving me,
    so far from my words of groaning?
²I cry out by day, O my God,
    but You do not answer,
    and by night,
    but I have no rest.
³Yet You are holy,
    enthroned on the praises of Israel.
⁴In You our fathers trusted;
    they trusted and You delivered them.
⁵They cried out to You and were set free;
    they trusted in You and were not
    disappointed.
⁶But I am a worm and not a man,
    scorned by men and despised by the people.
⁷All who see me mock me;
    they sneer and shake their heads:
⁸"He trusts in the LORD,
    let the LORD deliver him;
    let the LORD rescue him,
    since He delights in him."
⁹Yet You brought me out of the womb;
    You secured me at my mother's breast.
¹⁰From birth I was cast upon You;
    from my mother's womb You have been my
    God.
¹¹Be not far from me,
    for trouble is near
    and there is no one to help.
¹²Many bulls surround me;
    strong bulls of Bashan encircle me.
¹³They open their jaws against me
    like lions that roar and maul.
¹⁴I am poured out like water,

Psalm 22

    and all my bones are disjointed.
    My heart is like wax;
    it melts away within me.
[15]My strength is dried up like a potsherd,
    and my tongue sticks to the roof of my mouth.
    You lay me in the dust of death.
[16]For dogs surround me;
    a band of evil men encircles me;
    they have pierced my hands and feet.
[17]I can count all my bones;
    they stare and gloat over me.
[18]They divide my garments among them
    and cast lots for my clothing.
[19]But You, O LORD, be not far off;
    O my strength, come quickly to help.
[20]Deliver my soul from the sword,
    my precious life from the power of wild dogs.
[21]Save me from the mouth of the lion,
    at the horns of the wild oxen You have answered Me!
[22]I will proclaim Your name to my brothers;
    in the assembly I will praise You.
[23]You who fear the LORD, praise Him!
    All descendants of Jacob, honor Him!
    All offspring of Israel, revere Him!
[24]For He has not despised or detested
    the torment of the afflicted.
    He has not hidden His face from him,
    but has attended to his cry for help.
[25]From You comes my praise in the great assembly;
    before those who fear You I will fulfill my vows.
[26]The poor will eat and be satisfied;
    those who seek the LORD will praise Him.
    May your hearts live forever!
[27]All the ends of the earth

Psalm 22

    will remember and turn to the LORD.
All the families of the nations
    will bow down before Him.
[28] For dominion belongs to the LORD
    and He rules over the nations.
[29] All the rich of the earth will feast and worship;
    all who go down to the dust will kneel before Him—
    even those unable to preserve their lives.
[30] Posterity will serve Him;
    they will declare the Lord to a new generation.
[31] They will come and proclaim His righteousness
    to a people yet unborn—
    all that He has done.

    Psalm 22 is among the most misunderstood of all the Psalms, as lines of it are taken out of context, often in blasphemous ways. This is known as the Psalm of the Suffering Servant, and the first lines are not to say that the servant is suffering, but that the world mis-interprets the Servant's life as suffering. When not read in its entirety, the psalm seems to ask why God is unfaithful, which is blasphemy, when it is the people who do not see God's plan in the world, and are thus unfaithful to God.

    This psalm was written to comfort those who are oppressed and fear that God has abandoned them. But God is always faithful, always loving to those who have faith. (See Deuteronomy 7:9 and 2 Timothy 2:13 for examples of guarantees that God is always faithful.) This Psalm is one that presages Christ, and if not taken in context, would mean that Christ was abandoned by the Father if we did not read further and see that the central idea is that God has answered the plaintiff, showing that God has already won the battle, and that nothing can stop the plans of God. There is nothing that has ever existed or that will ever exist

Psalm 22

that can work against God effectively. Instead of seeming to be defeated, the use of these words by Christ were to proclaim to all those who knew their psalms that God was active and that no matter what the circumstances seemed at the moment, God was in control and would be victorious. We just need to have faith that no matter what our circumstances are, God is in control and all is part of the plan to bring further Glory to Him.

Questions to ask:
- Which of the words, lines, or ideas do you recognize from Masonic Work? (Remember to not write them down)
- How do these words, lines, or ideas take the meaning of the degrees and Masonic work and focus them to help make our lives more fit for the Builder's purpose and be Good Men and Masons?
- How do these words, lines, or ideas build our Faith in the Great Architect of the Universe?
- Which of these words, lines, or ideas OTHER than what is used in your Masonic jurisdiction help you to maintain your integrity and work for peace and justice?
- Discuss how these lines could be misunderstood or taken for other purposes that do not glorify God or help you grow as Masons.

NOTES:

Psalm 23

[1] The Lord is my shepherd; I shall not want.
[2] He maketh me to lie down in green pastures: he leadeth me beside the still waters.
[3] He restoreth my soul: he leadeth me in the paths of righteousness for his name's sake.
[4] Yea, though I walk through the valley of the shadow of death, I will fear no evil: for thou art with me; thy rod and thy staff they comfort me.
[5] Thou preparest a table before me in the presence of mine enemies: thou anointest my head with oil; my cup runneth over.
[6] Surely goodness and mercy shall follow me all the days of my life: and I will dwell in the house of the Lord for ever.

Psalm 23 is not about death, but about life. This Psalm was not written for the funerals at which it is so often read. In fact, the Psalm only began to be used for funerals after the printing of the 1928 Book of Common Prayer, but many different denominations of Christianity began to use it for funerals after that. The only line that refers at all to death is an allusion to the Valley of the shadow of death, but God is protecting from death there. Because it has become so tightly entwined with funerals, it would be impossible to change its use, but we can expand by considering more. It is essential to look at this psalm in terms of what it was originally supposed to function as. This psalm is about life.

The opening line tells us that this is about life by referring to the Lord as my shepherd. This says shepherd, not undertaker or butcher or cook. A shepherd takes care of the living and keeps them alive. Lying down in green pastures is a wonderful, benevolent activity for sheep, as they get to eat lush grass and are safe. Still waters can be

Psalm 23

drunk from without fear of being pulled into raging torrents and swept away. If you are safe and fed and with your flock and family, life is blessed and good. Your tables are overflowing with food and your life has been anointed with the oil of joy.

There are times of life that are struggles. Evil will threaten us in this Fallen world, and evil can be like a valley that holds many dangers like wolves and bears that we cannot see in the darkness of shadow. However, God is always with us. He is a good shepherd, taking active interest in every one of His sheep. His rod gently goads and pushes us in the right direction away from danger, and His staff is ready to defend us from whatever wild animal tries to attack us. Knowing that we are protected by such a good shepherd is a great comfort to all of us. We are not alone. We are cared for and loved. There in the middle of verse four, a transition takes place. The psalmist has been talking in the first person about himself, then he switches to talking directly to God using the term "thou." You, God, are with me protecting me.

After this switch in speech, the psalmist describes how much as a person God is doing for him. No matter what is happening in life, God is providing for us, even if we do not see. If we have faith in God, we can stop and partake of God's bounty and trust Him to take care of our enemies, at least until we are refreshed. God wants us to live good lives, but is not going to force us to live as He commands. If He did that, it would mean that we had no free will, and if we have no free will, our love for Him is meaningless, as we would have no choice. We are not really sheep, but loving beings made in His image. So, he gives us a choice and opens up options for us to trust in Him and love Him, and as our faith grows, we can start to understand more and more of life.

Look at 1 Corinthians 10:12-14 (NIV):

> [12] So, if you think you are standing firm, be careful that you don't fall! [13] No temptation has overtaken you except what is common

to mankind. And God is faithful; he will not let you be tempted beyond what you can bear. But when you are tempted, he will also provide a way out so that you can endure it. [14] Therefore, my dear friends, flee from idolatry."

Too often this is misquoted as "God will never give you more than you can handle." Of course this is not what is being said. God will not break your faith, only you do that. However, He will sometimes let you break your own heart. At times we are not focused on loving Him and one another. When we do not focus on love, we become idolaters focused on other gods, whether money or power or sex or anything else. When we recognize this, our hearts break in a good way: Psalm 51:17 tells us that: "My sacrifice, O God, is a broken spirit; a broken and contrite heart you, God, will not despise." This is saying that when we are humbled from rebelling against God, we can have a well-broken heart that is strengthened to believe in Him more and stop being idolatrous. This is where verse 3 of Psalm 23 is so poignant, as He restores my soul from being broken by sin.

If we live lives of faith and love, goodness and mercy will indeed follow you the rest of your life, and your life will be eternal. The Scriptures are clear about what this means. First, in Mark 12:30, Jesus quoted Deuteronomy 6:5: "And thou shalt love the LORD thy God with all thine heart, and with all thy soul, and with all thy might." Second, Leviticus 19:18 tells us "Do not seek revenge or bear a grudge against anyone among your people, but love your neighbor as yourself." This is also quoted directly by Jesus in Mark 12:31. If we do these things, there can be no alternatives but God's goodness and mercy will be with your faith the rest of our lives.

Questions to ask:

Psalm 23

- Which of the words, lines, or ideas do you recognize from Masonic Work? (Remember to not write them down)
- How do these words, lines, or ideas take the meaning of the degrees and Masonic work and focus them to help make our lives more fit for the Builder's purpose and be Good Men and Masons?
- How do these words, lines, or ideas build our Faith in the Great Architect of the Universe?
- Which of these words, lines, or ideas OTHER than what is used in your Masonic jurisdiction help you to maintain your integrity and work for peace and justice?
- Discuss how these lines could be misunderstood or taken for other purposes that do not glorify God or help you grow as Masons.

NOTES:

Psalm 25

[1] In you, Lord my God, I put my trust.
[2] I trust in you; do not let me be put to shame, nor let my enemies triumph over me.
[3] No one who hopes in you will ever be put to shame,
but shame will come on those who are treacherous without cause.
[4] Show me your ways, Lord, teach me your paths.
[5] Guide me in your truth and teach me, for you are God my Savior,
and my hope is in you all day long.
[6] Remember, Lord, your great mercy and love, for they are from of old.
[7] Do not remember the sins of my youth and my rebellious ways;
according to your love remember me, for you, Lord, are good.
[8] Good and upright is the Lord; therefore he instructs sinners in his ways.
[9] He guides the humble in what is right and teaches them his way.
[10] All the ways of the Lord are loving and faithful toward those who keep the demands of his covenant.
[11] For the sake of your name, Lord, forgive my iniquity, though it is great.
[12] Who, then, are those who fear the Lord? He will instruct them in the ways they should choose.
[13] They will spend their days in prosperity, and their descendants will inherit the land.
[14] The Lord confides in those who fear him; he makes his covenant known to them.
[15] My eyes are ever on the Lord, for only he will release my feet from the snare.

Psalm 25

> [16] Turn to me and be gracious to me, for I am lonely and afflicted.
> [17] Relieve the troubles of my heart and free me from my anguish.
> [18] Look on my affliction and my distress and take away all my sins.
> [19] See how numerous are my enemies and how fiercely they hate me!
> [20] Guard my life and rescue me; do not let me be put to shame, for I take refuge in you.
> [21] May integrity and uprightness protect me, because my hope, Lord, is in you.
> [22] Deliver Israel, O God, from all their troubles!

The first line sets the stage for this psalm, as it is not discussing a simple, momentary idea of putting faith in God, but placing faith in the Lord for the author's whole life, which is certainly an ideal stressed in Masonry. While many lines should seem familiar to Masons in lots of jurisdictions, many of these lines are used in many different degrees in not only Blue Lodge, but in York Rite and Scottish Rite work. Unfortunately, this psalm loses some of its beauty in translation to English. This psalm is an acrostic poem, the verses of which begin with the successive letters of the Hebrew alphabet.

Among the psalms, this is considered a relationship psalm, teaching of the relationship between God and humanity, and that while God might remember how badly we have sinned, He is loving. Some have called this a psalm of distress, as many of the other first 40 or so psalms are, yet it is also a psalm of great hope and faith. Even in a troubled and uncertain world, God is sure and Just. Psalms 24 and 26 are considered "ethics" psalms, but Psalm 25 has not been considered such, even though it deals with ethics in subtle ways. Some also classify these psalms (22&25) as individual lament psalms, singing of the worst part of

Psalm 25

peoples' lives, that of others not sharing the faith and love of God.

Questions to ask:
- Which of the words, lines, or ideas do you recognize from Masonic Work? (Remember to not write them down)
- How do these words, lines, or ideas take the meaning of the degrees and Masonic work and focus them to help make our lives more fit for the Builder's purpose and be Good Men and Masons?
- How do these words, lines, or ideas build our Faith in the Great Architect of the Universe?
- Which of these words, lines, or ideas OTHER than what is used in your Masonic jurisdiction help you to maintain your integrity and work for peace and justice?
- Discuss how these lines could be misunderstood or taken for other purposes that do not glorify God or help you grow as Masons.

NOTES:

Psalm 27

27 The LORD is my light and my salvation; whom shall I fear? the LORD is the strength of my life; of whom shall I be afraid?

² When the wicked, even mine enemies and my foes, came upon me to eat up my flesh, they stumbled and fell.

³ Though an host should encamp against me, my heart shall not fear: though war should rise against me, in this will I be confident.

⁴ One thing have I desired of the LORD, that will I seek after; that I may dwell in the house of the LORD all the days of my life, to behold the beauty of the LORD, and to enquire in his temple.

⁵ For in the time of trouble he shall hide me in his pavilion: in the secret of his tabernacle shall he hide me; he shall set me up upon a rock.

⁶ And now shall mine head be lifted up above mine enemies round about me: therefore will I offer in his tabernacle sacrifices of joy; I will sing, yea, I will sing praises unto the LORD.

⁷ Hear, O LORD, when I cry with my voice: have mercy also upon me, and answer me.

⁸ When thou saidst, Seek ye my face; my heart said unto thee, Thy face, LORD, will I seek.

⁹ Hide not thy face far from me; put not thy servant away in anger: thou hast been my help; leave me not, neither forsake me, O God of my salvation.

¹⁰ When my father and my mother forsake me, then the LORD will take me up.

¹¹ Teach me thy way, O LORD, and lead me in a plain path, because of mine enemies.

¹² Deliver me not over unto the will of mine enemies: for false witnesses are risen up against me, and such as breathe out cruelty.

Psalm 27

¹³ I had fainted, unless I had believed to see the goodness of the LORD in the land of the living.
¹⁴ Wait on the LORD: be of good courage, and he shall strengthen thine heart: wait, I say, on the LORD.

In the scriptures, rarely do we find such a beautiful and grand statement of faith as here, where the Lord is light and salvation. The Latin of St. Jerome's Vulgate, *"Dominus illuminatio mea,"* is the motto of the University of Oxford, simply because of the force of this statement (and the beauty of the poem). In many places God is analogized to Light, a personal favorite being Psalm 36:9: "In thy light we shall find light." In a few places the sentiment is closely related, such as John 1:7-9; John 12:35, 36, 46; 1 John 1:5. The Psalmist wants to be in the Tabernacle (later the Temple) as a place closest to God, and where he must be ritually pure, but also pure in heart and mind. While the Tabernacle might seem a poor hiding place from worldly enemies, David sings of the spiritual strength of being with God. While someone might rip through the curtains of the physical tabernacle, they cannot get through the protection afforded by true faith in God. Evan our earthly parents might not be enough to support our faith, which is where faith must be independent of humans, and entirely reliant on God. In the Reformation, this was discussed as salvation by Faith alone, through Grace alone, and by the Scriptures alone (*sola fides*, *sola gratias*, and *sola scritura*).[6]

When we have spiritual strength, we have patience. When we are weak in our faith, we get anxious and worried that God might not be moving fast enough. Technically, this is blasphemy, a word we are often loath to use in the

---

[6] There were two other "solas" in the Reformation: Solus Christus or Solo Christo ("Christ alone" or "through Christ alone") and Soli Deo gloria ("glory to God alone"), but those may not be considered evident in this passage.

Psalm 27

modern era. Faith in God is not faith in ourselves. When we say that God is moving too slowly for us, we are saying that our plans are better than God's plans, and we are the true Light of heaven. All light comes from God, whether physical light from His creation, spiritual Light of awareness of God, or the light of knowledge. A companion to this Psalm is Proverbs 2:6-8, which here is taken from the Contemporary English Version:

> [6] All wisdom comes from the Lord,
> and so do common sense
> and understanding.
> [7] God gives helpful advice
> to everyone who obeys him
> and protects all of those
> who live as they should.
> [8] God sees that justice is done,
> and he watches over everyone
> who is faithful to him.

As Masons, we seek Light, and this is in all of the senses described above, and for the reasons given in this Proverb. Only God can truly teach us His ways, but a brotherhood of men devoted to God can make the journey easier.

Questions to ask:

- Which of the words, lines, or ideas do you recognize from Masonic Work? (Remember to not write them down)
- How do these words, lines, or ideas take the meaning of the degrees and Masonic work and focus them to help make our lives more fit for the Builder's purpose and be Good Men and Masons?
- How do these words, lines, or ideas build our Faith in the Great Architect of the Universe?

Psalm 27

- Which of these words, lines, or ideas OTHER than what is used in your Masonic jurisdiction help you to maintain your integrity and work for peace and justice?
- Discuss how these lines could be misunderstood or taken for other purposes that do not glorify God or help you grow as Masons.

NOTES:

Psalm 46

¹ God is our refuge and strength, a very present help in trouble.
² Therefore will not we fear, though the earth be removed, and though the mountains be carried into the midst of the sea;
³ Though the waters thereof roar and be troubled, though the mountains shake with the swelling thereof. Selah.
⁴ There is a river, the streams whereof shall make glad the city of God, the holy place of the tabernacles of the most High.
⁵ God is in the midst of her; she shall not be moved: God shall help her, and that right early.
⁶ The heathen raged, the kingdoms were moved: he uttered his voice, the earth melted.
⁷ The LORD of hosts is with us; the God of Jacob is our refuge. Selah.
⁸ Come, behold the works of the LORD, what desolations he hath made in the earth.
⁹ He maketh wars to cease unto the end of the earth; he breaketh the bow, and cutteth the spear in sunder; he burneth the chariot in the fire.
¹⁰ Be still, and know that I am God: I will be exalted among the heathen, I will be exalted in the earth.
¹¹ The LORD of hosts is with us; the God of Jacob is our refuge. Selah.

It is sometimes difficult to hear this Psalm without singing along using Martin Luther's hymn that uses these words from this psalm. This psalm is also called a Song of Zion, written for public worship. It is always important to link the psalms to other places in scripture where ideas are manifest, such as how this psalm is an answer to the prayer

Psalm 46

of Isaiah 33:2, "Be thou their arm every morning, our salvation also in the time of trouble." Even if the Earth itself is torn apart, God is there for us, protecting us from all assaults. Where is our faith best founded? In the security of knowing God.

    This psalm begins with a parenthetic statement that it is "To the chief Musician for the sons of Korah, A Song upon Alamoth." Anything charged to the Chief Musician is to be sung by the most skilled, such that it can use its beauty best to praise God and instill its message into the hearts of believers. The sons of Korah had been spared when their father and all his company, and all the children of his associates were swallowed up alive in their sin in Numbers 27:11. These sons and their descendents were considered set aside to the constant praise and worship of God since they had been delivered by sovereign grace. The sins of the fathers were not visited on them, and they learned to put their pure faith in God.

    There is the next line describing this psalm as "A Song upon Alamoth." This term may denote that the music was to be pitched high for the treble or soprano voices of young Hebrew boys learning to be priests at the Tabernacle and Temple. We need to praise God with pure, childlike hearts and the enthusiasm that children often display when singing joyfully. Some interpreters have suggested that "Alamoth" might refer to shrill-sounding instruments, as in 1 Chronicles 15:20 , where we read that Zechariah, and Eliab, and Benaiah were to praise the Lord "with psalteries on Alamoth."

Questions to ask:
- Which of the words, lines, or ideas do you recognize from Masonic Work? (Remember to not write them down)
- How do these words, lines, or ideas take the meaning of the degrees and Masonic work and

Psalm 46

    focus them to help make our lives more fit for the Builder's purpose and be Good Men and Masons?
- How do these words, lines, or ideas build our Faith in the Great Architect of the Universe?
- Which of these words, lines, or ideas OTHER than what is used in your Masonic jurisdiction help you to maintain your integrity and work for peace and justice?
- Discuss how these lines could be misunderstood or taken for other purposes that do not glorify God or help you grow as Masons.

NOTES:

Psalm 90

[1] Lord, thou hast been our dwelling place in all generations.
[2] Before the mountains were brought forth, or ever thou hadst formed the earth and the world, even from everlasting to everlasting, thou art God.
[3] Thou turnest man to destruction; and sayest, Return, ye children of men.
[4] For a thousand years in thy sight are but as yesterday when it is past, and as a watch in the night.
[5] Thou carriest them away as with a flood; they are as a sleep: in the morning they are like grass which groweth up.
[6] In the morning it flourisheth, and groweth up; in the evening it is cut down, and withereth.
[7] For we are consumed by thine anger, and by thy wrath are we troubled.
[8] Thou hast set our iniquities before thee, our secret sins in the light of thy countenance.
[9] For all our days are passed away in thy wrath: we spend our years as a tale that is told.
[10] The days of our years are threescore years and ten; and if by reason of strength they be fourscore years, yet is their strength labour and sorrow; for it is soon cut off, and we fly away.
[11] Who knoweth the power of thine anger? even according to thy fear, so is thy wrath.
[12] So teach us to number our days, that we may apply our hearts unto wisdom.
[13] Return, O LORD, how long? and let it repent thee concerning thy servants.
[14] O satisfy us early with thy mercy; that we may rejoice and be glad all our days.

Psalm 90

> [15] Make us glad according to the days wherein thou hast afflicted us, and the years wherein we have seen evil.
> [16] Let thy work appear unto thy servants, and thy glory unto their children.
> [17] And let the beauty of the LORD our God be upon us: and establish thou the work of our hands upon us; yea, the work of our hands establish thou it.

This psalm is considered a Psalm of Moses, as the opening parenthesis says before the Psalm begins. While most acknowledge that the Psalms were written by David, here he may have recorded a song sung by his ancestors, perhaps even written by Moses. This is a song of a people living in the desert, wandering and far from the life they expected. People did not expect to live to be seventy, and rarely eighty. We cannot number God's days as our own, as God is eternal, and thus a thousand ages are like a moment. The question put here is what do we do with the time that we have?

What does it mean to dwell in the Lord? It means to focus on the rules for life that God has given us, and to consider what we are really supposed to be doing. Some Lodges even quote Micah 6:8:

> He has shown you, O mortal, what is good.
> And what does the LORD require of you?
> To act justly and to love mercy and to walk humbly with your God.

Psalm 90 is telling us to live faithful lives, worrying about spiritual matters like mercy above physical matters, and releasing out jealousy and hatred. Brotherhood cannot exist where hatred has taken hold. If we attempt to live without mercy, those days allotted to us are not going to be days that are worth living.

Psalm 90

Questions to ask:
- Which of the words, lines, or ideas do you recognize from Masonic Work? (Remember to not write them down)
- How do these words, lines, or ideas take the meaning of the degrees and Masonic work and focus them to help make our lives more fit for the Builder's purpose and be Good Men and Masons?
- How do these words, lines, or ideas build our Faith in the Great Architect of the Universe?
- Which of these words, lines, or ideas OTHER than what is used in your Masonic jurisdiction help you to maintain your integrity and work for peace and justice?
- Discuss how these lines could be misunderstood or taken for other purposes that do not glorify God or help you grow as Masons.

NOTES:

Psalm 103:13-22

[13] Like as a father pitieth his children, so the LORD pitieth them that fear him.
[14] For he knoweth our frame; he remembereth that we are dust.
[15] As for man, his days are as grass: as a flower of the field, so he flourisheth.
[16] For the wind passeth over it, and it is gone; and the place thereof shall know it no more.
[17] But the mercy of the LORD is from everlasting to everlasting upon them that fear him, and his righteousness unto children's children;
[18] To such as keep his covenant, and to those that remember his commandments to do them.
[19] The LORD hath prepared his throne in the heavens; and his kingdom ruleth over all.
[20] Bless the LORD, ye his angels, that excel in strength, that do his commandments, hearkening unto the voice of his word.
[21] Bless ye the LORD, all ye his hosts; ye ministers of his, that do his pleasure.
[22] Bless the LORD, all his works in all places of his dominion: bless the LORD, O my soul.

This psalm is a hymn of praise, called a doxology. Although mankind is, in many ways, inconsequential in creation, we are of utmost importance to God, who treats us as a loving father. God has love and pity for all of us. While it is difficult for many of us, scripture reinforces again and again that God's love is overwhelming and for all people, even those who are not good and who will receive punishment. Love is the blessing that cannot be contained. Those who keep faith with God will have rewards, but all have love that endures, even if our bodies become dust and ash, not much more than the grass or a flower. Life itself is

Psalm 103:13-22

uncertain for many people, and only the hope of the Lord's justice and mercy can give meaning to such fleeting lives.

Questions to ask:

- Which of the words, lines, or ideas do you recognize from Masonic Work? (Remember to not write them down)
- How do these words, lines, or ideas take the meaning of the degrees and Masonic work and focus them to help make our lives more fit for the Builder's purpose and be Good Men and Masons?
- How do these words, lines, or ideas build our Faith in the Great Architect of the Universe?
- Which of these words, lines, or ideas OTHER than what is used in your Masonic jurisdiction help you to maintain your integrity and work for peace and justice?
- Discuss how these lines could be misunderstood or taken for other purposes that do not glorify God or help you grow as Masons.

NOTES:

Psalm 115

¹ Not unto us, O Lord, not unto us, but unto thy name give glory, for thy mercy, and for thy truth's sake.

² Wherefore should the heathen say, Where is now their God?

³ But our God is in the heavens: he hath done whatsoever he hath pleased.

⁴ Their idols are silver and gold, the work of men's hands.

⁵ They have mouths, but they speak not: eyes have they, but they see not:

⁶ They have ears, but they hear not: noses have they, but they smell not:

⁷ They have hands, but they handle not: feet have they, but they walk not: neither speak they through their throat.

⁸ They that make them are like unto them; so is every one that trusteth in them.

⁹ O Israel, trust thou in the Lord: he is their help and their shield.

¹⁰ O house of Aaron, trust in the Lord: he is their help and their shield.

¹¹ Ye that fear the Lord, trust in the Lord: he is their help and their shield.

¹² The Lord hath been mindful of us: he will bless us; he will bless the house of Israel; he will bless the house of Aaron.

¹³ He will bless them that fear the Lord, both small and great.

¹⁴ The Lord shall increase you more and more, you and your children.

¹⁵ Ye are blessed of the Lord which made heaven and earth.

Psalm 115

¹⁶ The heaven, even the heavens, are the Lord's: but the earth hath he given to the children of men.
¹⁷ The dead praise not the Lord, neither any that go down into silence.
¹⁸ But we will bless the Lord from this time forth and for evermore. Praise the Lord.

    The opening phrase, recognizable to so many masons around the world, is a rejection of all forms of self-praise. Mercy and truth are references to the Covenant that God has made with the faithful. Other places in scripture have similar pleas, wherein God is asked to help us to find humility and remember His love (for example, in Daniel 9:18-19; Isaiah 48:9; Isaiah 48:11; Ezekiel 20:9; Ezekiel 20:14; and Ezekiel 36:21-23). We are not supposed to rely on our own merits or abilities to find grace, but rely on God and His Grace.
    When bad things happen to people of faith, non-believers may taunt us and ask us where God is in our pain. Faith is about understanding that you cannot always understand the fullness of God's plan, and that bad things can happen to good people, but that they are part of God's plan and not simply arbitrary elements of a chaos-filled world. God is with us, and He is living and real, not simply a piece of carved material made by human hands. We are made in God's image; He is not made in ours. God is a living, real, and the only god, not simply an idea.
    Verse 9 seems like an awkward transition, but this is a masterstroke of Hebrew poetry to allow for a song to be sung and change tune and rhythm so that the point is made. (remember that Psalms are inherently sung, not said. The word "psalm" comes from the word "*psallein*" (to pluck) and its derivative "*psalmos*" (a song sung to harp music). Here we have reiteration of the depth of blessing in the calls for Israel, the House of Aaron, and all who fear God, which are focusing inwards and outwards to include all people. For a

Psalm 115

Mason, this is a reminder that as important as humility is, faith is far more important.

The final two verses are a mystery for many people. We are not the first people to live, and we are not the only ones who have had faith. Those who have faith are promised life in God, but those who do not are in the place of silence, known as *Sheol* or *Hades*. We are alive, so therefore need to praise God, not the deeds of bygone days and heroic men.

Brother Rudyard Kipling referred to the elements of Psalm 115 in his poem **A School Song**, as he wrote of the antithesis of the psalm in how we over-rate humans, who are fallen and not always doing things for the best of reasons.

> 'Let us now praise famous men' -
> Men of little showing -
> For their work continueth,
> And their work continueth,
> Broad and deep continueth,
> Greater than their knowing!
>
> Western wind and open surge
> Took us from our mothers -
> Flung us on a naked shore
> (Twelve bleak houses by the shore.
> Seven summers by the shore!)
> 'Mid two hundred brothers.
>
> There we met with famous men
> Set in office o'er us;
> And they beat on us with rods -
> Faithfully with many rods -
> Daily beat us on with rods,
> For the love they bore us!
>
> Out of Egypt unto Troy -
> Over Himalaya -

Psalm 115

Far and sure our bands have gone -
Hy-Brazil or Babylon,
Islands of the Southern Run,
And Cities of Cathaia!

And we all praise famous men -
 Ancients of the College;
For they taught us common sense -
Tried to teach us common sense
Truth and God's Own Common Sense,
Which is more than knowledge!

Each degree of Latitude
 Strung about Creation
Seeth one or more of us
(Of one muster each of us),
Diligent in that he does,
Keen in his vocation.

This we learned from famous men,
Knowing not its uses,
When they showed, in daily work -
Man must finish off his work -
Right or wrong, his daily work -
And without excuses.

Servant of the Staff and chain,
Mine and fuse and grapnel -
Some, before the face of Kings,
Stand before the face of Kings;
Bearing gifts to divers Kings -
Gifts of case and shrapnel.

This we learned from famous men
Teaching in our borders,
Who declared it was best,
Safest, easiest, and best -

Psalm 115

> Expeditious, wise, and best -
> To obey your orders.
>
> Some beneath the further stars
>   Bear the greater burden:
> Set to serve the lands they rule,
> (Save he serve no man may rule),
> Serve and love the lands they rule;
> Seeking praise nor guerdon.
>
> This we learned from famous men,
>   Knowing not we learned it.
> Only, as the years went by -
> Lonely, as the years went by -
> Far from help as years went by,
> Plainer we discerned it.
>
> Wherefore praise we famous men
>   From whose bays we borrow -
> They that put aside To-day -
> All the joys of their To-day -
> And with toil of their To-day
>   Bought for us To-morrow!
>
> Bless and praise we famous men -
> Men of little showing -
> For their work continueth,
> And their work continueth,
> Broad and deep continueth,
> Great beyond their knowing!

Like the Psalm, if you do not read carefully, you might miss the point. Praise God, who deserves the glory, not men who seek the glory for themselves and will be gone as dust and whose names may not survive past their own lives.

Psalm 115

Questions to ask:

- Which of the words, lines, or ideas do you recognize from Masonic Work? (Remember to not write them down)
- How do these words, lines, or ideas take the meaning of the degrees and Masonic work and focus them to help make our lives more fit for the Builder's purpose and be Good Men and Masons?
- How do these words, lines, or ideas build our Faith in the Great Architect of the Universe?
- Which of these words, lines, or ideas OTHER than what is used in your Masonic jurisdiction help you to maintain your integrity and work for peace and justice?
- Discuss how these lines could be misunderstood or taken for other purposes that do not glorify God or help you grow as Masons.

NOTES:

Psalm 118

¹O give thanks unto the Lord; for he is good: because his mercy endureth for ever.
² Let Israel now say, that his mercy endureth for ever.
³ Let the house of Aaron now say, that his mercy endureth for ever.
⁴ Let them now that fear the Lord say, that his mercy endureth for ever.
⁵ I called upon the Lord in distress: the Lord answered me, and set me in a large place.
⁶ The Lord is on my side; I will not fear: what can man do unto me?
⁷ The Lord taketh my part with them that help me: therefore shall I see my desire upon them that hate me.
⁸ It is better to trust in the Lord than to put confidence in man.
⁹ It is better to trust in the Lord than to put confidence in princes.
¹⁰ All nations compassed me about: but in the name of the Lord will I destroy them.
¹¹ They compassed me about; yea, they compassed me about: but in the name of the Lord I will destroy them.
¹² They compassed me about like bees: they are quenched as the fire of thorns: for in the name of the Lord I will destroy them.
¹³ Thou hast thrust sore at me that I might fall: but the Lord helped me.
¹⁴ The Lord is my strength and song, and is become my salvation.
¹⁵ The voice of rejoicing and salvation is in the tabernacles of the righteous: the right hand of the Lord doeth valiantly.

Psalm 118

[16] The right hand of the Lord is exalted: the right hand of the Lord doeth valiantly.

[17] I shall not die, but live, and declare the works of the Lord.

[18] The Lord hath chastened me sore: but he hath not given me over unto death.

[19] Open to me the gates of righteousness: I will go into them, and I will praise the Lord:

[20] This gate of the Lord, into which the righteous shall enter.

[21] I will praise thee: for thou hast heard me, and art become my salvation.

[22] The stone which the builders refused is become the head stone of the corner.

[23] This is the Lord's doing; it is marvellous in our eyes.

[24] This is the day which the Lord hath made; we will rejoice and be glad in it.

[25] Save now, I beseech thee, O Lord: O Lord, I beseech thee, send now prosperity.

[26] Blessed be he that cometh in the name of the Lord: we have blessed you out of the house of the Lord.

[27] God is the Lord, which hath shewed us light: bind the sacrifice with cords, even unto the horns of the altar.

[28] Thou art my God, and I will praise thee: thou art my God, I will exalt thee.

[29] O give thanks unto the Lord; for he is good: for his mercy endureth for ever.

Psalm 118 has one of the most complex structures of any Psalm in the Bible. There are several sections of the overall song, and then several *chiasms*, or repeating balanced structures where comments start and end around a central concept. This psalm is part of a group of psalms from 113-118 that focus on praising God and recognizing that only

Psalm 118

through God can anything be accomplished, and to say that we have done anything without God is foolhardy at best.

The first thing that most people notice about this Psalm are the repetitions of "his mercy endureth for ever" in the first four lines and the final line. Rarely in the Psalms is something repeated as often as this phrase, which should enter into the hearts of the readers or hearers that this is the most essential aspect of the psalm. The second thing that English speakers will notice is the similarity of the lines:

> [8] It is better to trust in the Lord than to put confidence in man.
> [9] It is better to trust in the Lord than to put confidence in princes.

Man and prices cannot save, but only God can do this. Men and princes may be made in the image of God, but are not always acting in the image of God. This sets up ideas of the coming of the Messiah that have been discussed since.

What does not always appear in English is called a chiastic structure of the psalm. *Chi* is the Greek letter X, so a chiastic structure is one in which the top (beginning) and bottom (end) reflect and balance each other, and between this first and last other items match. In between the balanced portion is a central theme that the whole psalm or poem is trying to point you towards. A chiasm therefore is represented as:

1- beginning
    2- middle
        3-central theme
        3'- reiteration of central theme
    2'- counter-middle
1'- ending- counter beginning

Psalm 118

One suggested chiasm in Psalm 118 is:

1) verses 1-4, Oh give thanks to the LORD for He is good! For His mercy endures forever!
    2) verses 5-13, I called on the LORD in my distress;
        3) verse 14a, The LORD is my strength and song;
            4) verses 14b-16, The LORD my salvation + voice of rejoicing/ salvation/ righteous + right hand exalted;
                5/5') verses 17-18, "I shall not die, but live, and declare the works of the LORD. The LORD has chastened me severely, but He has not given me over to death
            4') verses 19-23, Praise/ gates of righteousness/ righteous + LORD my salvation + chief cornerstone;
        3') verse 24, This is the day the LORD has made; we will rejoice and be glad in it;
    2') verses 25-28, Save now, I pray, O LORD;
1') verse 29, Oh give thanks to the LORD for He is good! For His mercy endures forever!

Although verse 24 (This is the day the LORD has made; we will rejoice and be glad in it) is the most widely known verse in this psalm, the central theme really is the theme appearing in verses 17-18, "I shall not die, but live, and declare the works of the LORD. The LORD has chastened me severely, but He has not given me over to death.

Another way to examine the psalm is to break down some of the themes in it into another chiastic structure. For example, major themes include:

Psalm 118

1) Praise to YHWH *(verses 1-4)*
    2) the Messiah Trusts in YHWH *(verses 5-9)*
        3) the Messiah will be surrounded by his enemies *(verses 10-13)*
            4/4') the Messiah will be victorious *(verses 14-16)*
        3') the Messiah will be resurrected *(verses 17-21)*
    2') the Messiah will be recognized by all people *(verses 22-27)*
1') the Messiah will praise YHWH forever *(verses 28-29)*

In this case, the central theme is that the Messiah will be victorious, which is very closely related to the central theme above in the other chiastic interpretation.

Questions to ask:
- Which of the words, lines, or ideas do you recognize from Masonic Work? (Remember to not write them down)
- How do these words, lines, or ideas take the meaning of the degrees and Masonic work and focus them to help make our lives more fit for the Builder's purpose and be Good Men and Masons?
- How do these words, lines, or ideas build our Faith in the Great Architect of the Universe?
- Which of these words, lines, or ideas OTHER than what is used in your Masonic jurisdiction help you to maintain your integrity and work for peace and justice?
- Discuss how these lines could be misunderstood or taken for other purposes that do not glorify God or help you grow as Masons.

NOTES:

Psalm 121

¹ I will lift up mine eyes unto the hills, from whence cometh my help.
² My help cometh from the LORD, which made heaven and earth.
³ He will not suffer thy foot to be moved: he that keepeth thee will not slumber.
⁴ Behold, he that keepeth Israel shall neither slumber nor sleep.
⁵ The LORD is thy keeper: the LORD is thy shade upon thy right hand.
⁶ The sun shall not smite thee by day, nor the moon by night.
⁷ The LORD shall preserve thee from all evil: he shall preserve thy soul.
⁸ The LORD shall preserve thy going out and thy coming in from this time forth, and even for evermore.

The Psalmist is looking to the hills upon which Jerusalem is built, and where will one day stand the Temple of God. Some of the Canaanites worshipped the land itself, and this psalm refutes their claims and focuses attention on YHWH, the Lord God of Israel. Faith in God is the essential characteristic of this psalm, focusing on the realities of how much God helps us and how little we have to fear from anything if our faith is well founded in Him.

As in other Hebrew poems, the reiteration of slumber is an assurance that God is paying attention. In one of the funniest lines in the Old Testament, 1 Kings 18:27, Elijah makes fun of Baal and those who worship Baal during a competition to see whose god is best:

> ²⁷At noon Elijah began to taunt them. "Shout louder!" he said. "Surely he is a god! Perhaps he is

Psalm 121

deep in thought, or busy, or traveling. Maybe he is sleeping and must be awakened."

This might not seem as funny in English, but what Elijah is doing is showing that if their gods exist, which is demonstrated to be false, they are not attentive to those worshipping them. Elijah is directly implying that if Baal exists, he is too busy on the toilet to worry about his followers. When we translate the Bible, we tend to avoid toilet humor, but it is there. God, however, cares deeply for us and takes care of us.

Questions to ask:
- Which of the words, lines, or ideas do you recognize from Masonic Work? (Remember to not write them down)
- How do these words, lines, or ideas take the meaning of the degrees and Masonic work and focus them to help make our lives more fit for the Builder's purpose and be Good Men and Masons?
- How do these words, lines, or ideas build our Faith in the Great Architect of the Universe?
- Which of these words, lines, or ideas OTHER than what is used in your Masonic jurisdiction help you to maintain your integrity and work for peace and justice?
- Discuss how these lines could be misunderstood or taken for other purposes that do not glorify God or help you grow as Masons.

Psalm 121

NOTES:

Psalm 122

¹A Song of ascents. Of David.
>I was glad when they said to me,
>>"Let us go to the house of the LORD."

²Our feet are standing in your gates,
>O Jerusalem.

³Jerusalem is built up
>as a city united together,

⁴where the tribes go up,
>the tribes of the LORD,
>as a testimony for Israel,
>to give thanks to the name of the LORD.

⁵For there the thrones of judgment stand,
>the thrones of the house of David.

⁶Pray for the peace of Jerusalem:
>"May those who love you prosper.

⁷May there be peace within your walls,
>and prosperity inside your fortresses."

⁸For the sake of my brothers and friends,
>I will say, "Peace be within you."

⁹For the sake of the house of the LORD our God,
>I will seek your prosperity.

Many brethren, especially British masons and Anglophiles, will know that this is the coronation anthem used by British royalty, set to music by Hubert Parry. Among the most hauntingly beautiful settings of a psalm, it is sung now just as then, focusing on the great joy of God's blessings. Jerusalem, the city of peace, is where God reigns above all, and where humanity seeks the promises of God in the richest blessings (see also Psalm 133). Jerusalem is a model for future kings and queens, as it is the place from which God's Word came, and radiates out to all other people. We are told to pray for the peace of Jerusalem so that we can all attain the unity that comes from the Peace of

Psalm 122

God. It is not simply the peace of Jerusalem that matters, but Jerusalem (which literally means "*City of Peace*") is representative of the whole world. When we pray for peace ther, we are praying for the entirety of the Kingdom of God.

Questions to ask:
- Which of the words, lines, or ideas do you recognize from Masonic Work? (Remember to not write them down)
- How do these words, lines, or ideas take the meaning of the degrees and Masonic work and focus them to help make our lives more fit for the Builder's purpose and be Good Men and Masons?
- How do these words, lines, or ideas build our Faith in the Great Architect of the Universe?
- Which of these words, lines, or ideas OTHER than what is used in your Masonic jurisdiction help you to maintain your integrity and work for peace and justice?
- Discuss how these lines could be misunderstood or taken for other purposes that do not glorify God or help you grow as Masons.

NOTES:

Psalm 133

¹Behold, how good and how pleasant it is for brethren to dwell together in unity! ²It is like the precious ointment upon the head, that ran down upon the beard, even Aaron's beard: that went down to the skirts of his garments; ³As the dew of Hermon, and as the dew that descended upon the mountains of Zion: for there the Lord commanded the blessing, even life for evermore.

In this passage, the beauty and richness of God's blessings are made evident. Brethren here are not from a single family, but from an extended and adopted family, as when the tribes came back to Jerusalem for Feasts and festivals. When we get along, we are not wasting time and effort, and we are acting more in the image of God that we were intended to. Living together in peace and unity where we listen to each other well is a reminder of the origins of creation and Eden itself. It harkens back to the second chapter of Genesis:

Genesis 2
¹⁸Then the LORD God said, "It is not good for the man to be alone; I will make him a helper suitable for him." ¹⁹Out of the ground the LORD God formed every beast of the field and every bird of the sky, and brought *them* to the man to see what he would call them; and whatever the man called a living creature, that was its name. ²⁰The man gave names to all the cattle, and to the birds of the sky, and to every beast of the field, but for Adam there was not found a helper suitable for him. ²¹So the LORD God caused a deep sleep to fall upon the man, and he slept; then He took one of his ribs and closed up the flesh at that place. ²²The LORD God

Psalm 133

> fashioned into a woman the rib which He had taken from the man, and brought her to the man.
> ²³The man said,
>> "This is now bone of my bones,
>> And flesh of my flesh;
>> She shall be called Woman,
>> Because she was taken out of Man."

God intends for us to live in community. We are supposed to live together and love one another as members of God's family. And when we live together, we share God's blessings and represent them well. Unity and brotherly love is represented in verse 2 as the precious sacramental ointment of the priests. Normally, the priests would be given a ritual anointing with a small amount of this oil with its very expensive spices. When Aaron was made High Priest, it was poured over his head, representing how much God showers blessings on those who love him and follow his commandments. In this passage, God's blessings on Aaron are almost wasteful in the generosity, as all of those blessings are extraneous, as even a little of God's blessings are enough to change the world. Here, from Exodus 30:22-33 (NIV) is the description of the Anointing Oil:

> ²²Then the Lord said to Moses, ²³"Take the following fine spices: 500 shekels[7] of liquid myrrh, half as much (that is, 250 shekels) of fragrant cinnamon, 250 shekels[8] of fragrant calamus, ²⁴500 shekels of cassia—all according to the sanctuary shekel—and a hin[9] of olive oil. ²⁵ Make these into a sacred anointing oil, a fragrant blend, the work of a perfumer. It will be the sacred anointing oil. ²⁶Then use it to anoint the tent of meeting, the ark of the

---

[7] That is, about 12 1/2 pounds or about 5.8 kilograms; also in verse 24
[8] That is, about 6 1/4 pounds or about 2.9 kilograms
[9] That is, probably about 1 gallon or about 3.8 liters

Psalm 133

covenant law, ²⁷the table and all its articles, the lampstand and its accessories, the altar of incense, ²⁸the altar of burnt offering and all its utensils, and the basin with its stand.²⁹You shall consecrate them so they will be most holy, and whatever touches them will be holy. ³⁰"Anoint Aaron and his sons and consecrate them so they may serve me as priests. ³¹Say to the Israelites, 'This is to be my sacred anointing oil for the generations to come. ³²Do not pour it on anyone else's body and do not make any other oil using the same formula. It is sacred, and you are to consider it sacred. ³³Whoever makes perfume like it and puts it on anyone other than a priest must be cut off from their people.'"

In his commentary, Ellicott reminds us that this psalm was read at the reception of a new member into the brotherhood of the Knights Templars, and quoted by St. Augustine as the Divine authority for monastic life.

Questions to ask:
- Which of the words, lines, or ideas do you recognize from Masonic Work? (Remember to not write them down)
- How do these words, lines, or ideas take the meaning of the degrees and Masonic work and focus them to help make our lives more fit for the Builder's purpose and be Good Men and Masons?
- How do these words, lines, or ideas build our Faith in the Great Architect of the Universe?
- Which of these words, lines, or ideas OTHER than what is used in your Masonic jurisdiction help you to maintain your integrity and work for peace and justice?

Psalm 133
- Discuss how these lines could be misunderstood or taken for other purposes that do not glorify God or help you grow as Masons.

NOTES:

Psalm 141

¹ Lord, I cry unto thee: make haste unto me; give ear unto my voice, when I cry unto thee. ² Let my prayer be set forth before thee as incense; and the lifting up of my hands as the evening sacrifice. ³ Set a watch, O LORD, before my mouth; keep the door of my lips. ⁴ Incline not my heart to any evil thing, to practice wicked works with men that work iniquity: and let me not eat of their dainties. ⁵ Let the righteous smite me; it shall be a kindness: and let him reprove me; it shall be an excellent oil, which shall not break my head: for yet my prayer also shall be in their calamities. ⁶ When their judges are overthrown in stony places, they shall hear my words; for they are sweet. ⁷ Our bones are scattered at the grave's mouth, as when one cutteth and cleaveth wood upon the earth. ⁸ But mine eyes are unto thee, O GOD the Lord: in thee is my trust; leave not my soul destitute. ⁹ Keep me from the snares which they have laid for me, and the gins of the workers of iniquity. ¹⁰ Let the wicked fall into their own nets, whilst that I withal escape.

This psalm is an individual lament, whereby David tries to explain the calamities of his life. In spite of what he has experienced, David is still trying to relate the depth of faith that he has in God. He is recognizing that he does not keep himself from saying things that can get him into further trouble, and he actively wants to not desire evil actions, especially revenge and hurt. This is sometimes considered a reiteration of the Law, which is focused on mercy. An eye for an eye, for example, is a law limiting how much retribution you can take from a person who has

Psalm 141

wronged you. If someone takes out your eye, the most you are allowed to take is his eye, but you should not take his eye. Only if you cannot be faithful and show mercy should you take retribution, and then it must be limited.

Here in this Psalm, we have an implied tie to this, where David recognizes how easy it is to repay hatred with hatred. If David is to follow God, he must try to bear the image of God well and act as God would want him to. The same goes for us, and we too beg God to be merciful and release us from being vengeful such that we bear the pain of vengeance we inflict.

Questions to ask:

- Which of the words, lines, or ideas do you recognize from Masonic Work? (Remember to not write them down)
- How do these words, lines, or ideas take the meaning of the degrees and Masonic work and focus them to help make our lives more fit for the Builder's purpose and be Good Men and Masons?
- How do these words, lines, or ideas build our Faith in the Great Architect of the Universe?
- Which of these words, lines, or ideas OTHER than what is used in your Masonic jurisdiction help you to maintain your integrity and work for peace and justice?
- Discuss how these lines could be misunderstood or taken for other purposes that do not glorify God or help you grow as Masons.

NOTES:

Ecclesiastes 4:1-16

¹ So I returned, and considered all the oppressions that are done under the sun: and behold the tears of such as were oppressed, and they had no comforter; and on the side of their oppressors there was power; but they had no comforter. ² Wherefore I praised the dead which are already dead more than the living which are yet alive. ³ Yea, better is he than both they, which hath not yet been, who hath not seen the evil work that is done under the sun. ⁴ Again, I considered all travail, and every right work, that for this a man is envied of his neighbour. This is also vanity and vexation of spirit. ⁵ The fool foldeth his hands together, and eateth his own flesh. ⁶ Better is an handful with quietness, than both the hands full with travail and vexation of spirit. ⁷ Then I returned, and I saw vanity under the sun. ⁸ There is one alone, and there is not a second; yea, he hath neither child nor brother: yet is there no end of all his labour; neither is his eye satisfied with riches; neither saith he, For whom do I labour, and bereave my soul of good? This is also vanity, yea, it is a sore travail. ⁹ Two are better than one; because they have a good reward for their labour. ¹⁰ For if they fall, the one will lift up his fellow: but woe to him that is alone when he falleth; for he hath not another to help him up. ¹¹ Again, if two lie together, then they have heat: but how can one be warm alone? ¹² And if one prevail against him, two shall withstand him; and a threefold cord is not quickly broken. ¹³ Better is a poor and a wise child than an old and foolish king, who will no more be admonished. ¹⁴ For out of prison he cometh to reign; whereas also he that is born in his kingdom becometh poor. ¹⁵ I considered all the living which walk under the sun, with the second child that shall stand up in his stead. ¹⁶ There

Ecclesiastes 4:1-16

is no end of all the people, even of all that have been before them: they also that come after shall not rejoice in him. Surely this also is vanity and vexation of spirit.

The first three verses here are lamenting that *might* sometimes wins over *right*. Most people are familiar with the quote by Thucydides that "might *makes* right." There is unfairness in the world and the systems of the world can take a bad apple and spoil more than the barrel full. People do stupid things, and some would often rather fight just so that they feel alive because they have no faith in the one who gives them life. We are not made to be alone. God made us to be in company with one another, and when we have an arm to support us, the strength of that support eases our souls and helps us to worship God properly (and together!).

A threefold cord was a symbol of unity, whether friends or a family (father, mother, and children as strands). Three is a number of God, and as such the third part of the cord (the strongest ropes in existence at that time were three-stranded), represented something dedicated to God.

Questions to ask:
- Which of the words, lines, or ideas do you recognize from Masonic Work? (Remember to not write them down)
- How do these words, lines, or ideas take the meaning of the degrees and Masonic work and focus them to help make our lives more fit for the Builder's purpose and be Good Men and Masons?
- How do these words, lines, or ideas build our Faith in the Great Architect of the Universe?

Ecclesiastes 4:1-16
- Which of these words, lines, or ideas OTHER than what is used in your Masonic jurisdiction help you to maintain your integrity and work for peace and justice?
- Discuss how these lines could be misunderstood or taken for other purposes that do not glorify God or help you grow as Masons.

NOTES:

Ecclesiastes 12:1-14

¹ Remember now thy Creator in the days of thy youth, while the evil days come not, nor the years draw nigh, when thou shalt say, I have no pleasure in them; ² While the sun, or the light, or the moon, or the stars, be not darkened, nor the clouds return after the rain: ³ In the day when the keepers of the house shall tremble, and the strong men shall bow themselves, and the grinders cease because they are few, and those that look out of the windows be darkened, ⁴ And the doors shall be shut in the streets, when the sound of the grinding is low, and he shall rise up at the voice of the bird, and all the daughters of musick shall be brought low; ⁵ Also when they shall be afraid of that which is high, and fears shall be in the way, and the almond tree shall flourish, and the grasshopper shall be a burden, and desire shall fail: because man goeth to his long home, and the mourners go about the streets: ⁶ Or ever the silver cord be loosed, or the golden bowl be broken, or the pitcher be broken at the fountain, or the wheel broken at the cistern. ⁷ Then shall the dust return to the earth as it was: and the spirit shall return unto God who gave it. ⁸ Vanity of vanities, saith the preacher; all is vanity. ⁹ And moreover, because the preacher was wise, he still taught the people knowledge; yea, he gave good heed, and sought out, and set in order many proverbs. ¹⁰ The preacher sought to find out acceptable words: and that which was written was upright, even words of truth. ¹¹ The words of the wise are as goads, and as nails fastened by the masters of assemblies, which are given from one shepherd. ¹² And further, by these, my son, be admonished: of making many books there is no end; and much study is a weariness of the flesh. ¹³ Let us hear the conclusion

Ecclesiastes 12:1-14

of the whole matter: Fear God, and keep his commandments: for this is the whole duty of man. [14] For God shall bring every work into judgment, with every secret thing, whether it be good, or whether it be evil.

Among scripture, this is one of the most appropriate topics for youth today. It is common to hear young people say "I am spiritual, but not religious" or "I will worry about religion when I have children." The Preacher who wrote Ecclesiastes is directly combatting these two ideas with wisdom directly from God.

The various verses depict the ravages of old age, from failing eyesight and hearing to loss of teeth, from brittle bones to frail muscles. Life itself becomes difficult for people who have no pleasure and passion left. To see that life is about pleasure and not about focusing on the God who gave us life is vanity. To think that we can enjoy life and not give thanks to God who gave us life is vanity. To think that we made ourselves and are more than dust without the spirit that God has given to us, and therefore owing all to God, it also vanity. Only in full relationship with God as our creator, sustainer, and redeemer can we live in fullness and joy. To say that you are spiritual is to acknowledge that there is a god, and seeing the reality of God in our lives is overwhelming. Some might have such a view because they see evil in the church. There is evil anywhere that human beings are; we cannot put such offenses at God's feet. If we are to have free will, then the love we offer God has to be voluntary, and we only have free will if we have an option to not love God. Some will take that option. Some will not see the free offer of grace and love that comes from God. They will say that they do not need it while they are young and healthy. They see religion as only eternal fire insurance that might save them from hell.

As people get older and start to see their mortality, especially when they have children, this is when people start

Ecclesiastes 12:1-14

to see religion again as important. They want to have their children brought up in the church to teach them good lessons and have the same socialization that they did. While this is a wonderful outcome, it is the wrong reason. God is not simply there for questions of life and death, He is there for all questions of life, as He designed life. Verses 13 and 14 remind us that the chief purpose of humanity is to love God and worship Him. This is what we were made for, and not just for when we are older and facing our mortality, but for every day of our lives. Those who heed God and love Him with all their hearts and minds and strength are those who will see the beauty and love of resurrection and life eternal. Doing as we please and not believing until we put on a show later in life does not fool anyone, especially not the Architect of the Universe.

Questions to ask:
- Which of the words, lines, or ideas do you recognize from Masonic Work? (Remember to not write them down)
- How do these words, lines, or ideas take the meaning of the degrees and Masonic work and focus them to help make our lives more fit for the Builder's purpose and be Good Men and Masons?
- How do these words, lines, or ideas build our Faith in the Great Architect of the Universe?
- Which of these words, lines, or ideas OTHER than what is used in your Masonic jurisdiction help you to maintain your integrity and work for peace and justice?
- Discuss how these lines could be misunderstood or taken for other purposes that do not glorify God or help you grow as Masons.

Ecclesiastes 12:1-14

NOTES:

Isaiah 8:1-10

¹Moreover the LORD said unto me, Take thee a great roll, and write in it with a man's pen concerning Mahershalalhashbaz. ²And I took unto me faithful witnesses to record, Uriah the priest, and Zechariah the son of Jeberechiah. ³And I went unto the prophetess; and she conceived, and bare a son. Then said the LORD to me, Call his name Mahershalalhashbaz. ⁴For before the child shall have knowledge to cry, My father, and my mother, the riches of Damascus and the spoil of Samaria shall be taken away before the king of Assyria. ⁵The LORD spake also unto me again, saying, ⁶Forasmuch as this people refuseth the waters of Shiloah that go softly, and rejoice in Rezin and Remaliah's son; ⁷Now therefore, behold, the Lord bringeth up upon them the waters of the river, strong and many, *even* the king of Assyria, and all his glory: and he shall come up over all his channels, and go over all his banks: ⁸And he shall pass through Judah; he shall overflow and go over, he shall reach *even* to the neck; and the stretching out of his wings shall fill the breadth of thy land, O Immanuel. ⁹Associate yourselves, O ye people, and ye shall be broken in pieces; and give ear, all ye of far countries: gird yourselves, and ye shall be broken in pieces; gird yourselves, and ye shall be broken in pieces. ¹⁰Take counsel together, and it shall come to nought; speak the word, and it shall not stand: for God *is* with us.

Isaiah 8:1-10

Writing in about the eighth century B.C., Isaiah lived during the reigns of the four Kings of Judah[10]: Uzziah, Jotham, Ahaz, and Hezekiah (Isaiah 1:1). He was married to a woman that we know only as "the prophetess" (Isaiah 8:3). They had two sons Shear-jashub which means "*a remnant shall return*" (Isaiah 7:3) and Maher-Shalal-Hash-Baz which means "*spoil quickly, plunder speedily*" (Isaiah 8:3).

Fun trivia for many is that this is the longest name in the Bible: **Maher-shalal-hash-baz** (מהרשללחשבז), which is variously interpreted as meaning "quick to plunder and swift to spoil" or "he has made haste to the plunder!" His name represents what is happening to his people, being carried off as spoils of war and the plundered heart of the land. Contrast his name to the beginning of verse 9, which really should be translated by meaning: ***Do your Worst!*** It cries to those who would carry off Israel as if that could stop people from worshipping God. In fact, their worst helped restore faith to the children of Israel, who began to realize what God had been asking them to do for so long, but they had refused and become hard of heart. Verses 8 and 10 refer to Immanuel, which literally means ***God with us***, reminding the reader that no matter where we go, God is there.

Questions to ask:

- Which of the words, lines, or ideas do you recognize from Masonic Work? (Remember to not write them down)
- How do these words, lines, or ideas take the meaning of the degrees and Masonic work and focus them to help make our lives more fit for the Builder's purpose and be Good Men and Masons?

---

[10] Judah was also known as Zion at that time

Isaiah 8:1-10

- How do these words, lines, or ideas build our Faith in the Great Architect of the Universe?
- Which of these words, lines, or ideas OTHER than what is used in your Masonic jurisdiction help you to maintain your integrity and work for peace and justice?
- Discuss how these lines could be misunderstood or taken for other purposes that do not glorify God or help you grow as Masons.

NOTES:

Isaiah 42:1-25

¹ Behold my servant, whom I uphold; mine elect, in whom my soul delighteth; I have put my spirit upon him: he shall bring forth judgment to the Gentiles. ² He shall not cry, nor lift up, nor cause his voice to be heard in the street. ³ A bruised reed shall he not break, and the smoking flax shall he not quench: he shall bring forth judgment unto truth. ⁴ He shall not fail nor be discouraged, till he have set judgment in the earth: and the isles shall wait for his law. ⁵ Thus saith God the LORD, he that created the heavens, and stretched them out; he that spread forth the earth, and that which cometh out of it; he that giveth breath unto the people upon it, and spirit to them that walk therein: ⁶ I the LORD have called thee in righteousness, and will hold thine hand, and will keep thee, and give thee for a covenant of the people, for a light of the Gentiles; ⁷ To open the blind eyes, to bring out the prisoners from the prison, and them that sit in darkness out of the prison house. ⁸ I am the LORD: that is my name: and my glory will I not give to another, neither my praise to graven images. ⁹ Behold, the former things are come to pass, and new things do I declare: before they spring forth I tell you of them. ¹⁰ Sing unto the LORD a new song, and his praise from the end of the earth, ye that go down to the sea, and all that is therein; the isles, and the inhabitants thereof. ¹¹ Let the wilderness and the cities thereof lift up their voice, the villages that Kedar doth inhabit: let the inhabitants of the rock sing, let them shout from the top of the mountains. ¹² Let them give glory unto the LORD, and declare his praise in the islands. ¹³ The LORD shall go forth as a mighty man, he shall stir up jealousy like a man of war: he shall cry, yea, roar; he

Isaiah 42:1-25

shall prevail against his enemies. ¹⁴ I have long time holden my peace; I have been still, and refrained myself: now will I cry like a travailing woman; I will destroy and devour at once. ¹⁵ I will make waste mountains and hills, and dry up all their herbs; and I will make the rivers islands, and I will dry up the pools. ¹⁶ And I will bring the blind by a way that they knew not; I will lead them in paths that they have not known: I will make darkness light before them, and crooked things straight. These things will I do unto them, and not forsake them. ¹⁷ They shall be turned back, they shall be greatly ashamed, that trust in graven images, that say to the molten images, Ye are our gods. ¹⁸ Hear, ye deaf; and look, ye blind, that ye may see. ¹⁹ Who is blind, but my servant? or deaf, as my messenger that I sent? who is blind as he that is perfect, and blind as the LORD's servant? ²⁰ Seeing many things, but thou observest not; opening the ears, but he heareth not. ²¹ The LORD is well pleased for his righteousness' sake; he will magnify the law, and make it honourable. ²² But this is a people robbed and spoiled; they are all of them snared in holes, and they are hid in prison houses: they are for a prey, and none delivereth; for a spoil, and none saith, Restore. ²³ Who among you will give ear to this? who will hearken and hear for the time to come? ²⁴ Who gave Jacob for a spoil, and Israel to the robbers? did not the LORD, he against whom we have sinned? for they would not walk in his ways, neither were they obedient unto his law. ²⁵ Therefore he hath poured upon him the fury of his anger, and the strength of battle: and it hath set him on fire round about, yet he knew not; and it burned him, yet he laid it not to heart.

This section is divided into two subsections. First is God's promise concerning his servant, the messiah, in

Isaiah 42:1-25

verses 1-13. The second sub-section is the blindness of the people in verses 14-25. In the first verse is the word elect, which Isaiah introduces to Christian theology at this point which became a Reformed view of election picked up by Calvin. This remnant of Israel who are able to return from captivity, and are admonished to maintain humility. There should be gentleness and kindness, not breaking the bruised, not snuffing out those who are spiritually weak, but helping them shine brighter.

    The Messiah is supposed to stop evil and nourish good. We are supposed to emulate the Messiah and try to heal and nourish. Opening the eyes of the blind is to set free from the prison of self-centeredness or pride. This is where our worst graven images are: in our own hearts. If you were to ask what you truly love most in the world, and what you could not give up, if it is not God, then it is a graven image that you are worshipping. This idea of loving God more than anything or anyone else is difficult at times, especially with family members, whom we are supposed to love completely, but not more than we love God. This was the basis for the Law in Leviticus that people became enslaved to, but yet Isaiah, the Psalms, and Christ all tell us that the Law was to set us free, not bind us to slavish adherence. The Law is about mercy, including to self. The new song that should be sung is the new song of spiritual release from oppression, and the song of utter abandonment of self into the fullness of God.

    Verse 14 begins the second section, and in here is a change of person. Before it was Isaiah speaking, now he is writing the words from God's perspective. God has held Israel in safety, even if they only saw it as slavery. The people considered ignorant of God, gentiles and other unbelievers, are brought by ways they could not know, as they are ways of light and truth in God. We are turned back from our sinful ways and shown why they are sinful; how they distance us from God. Those who are deaf and blind may not have any physical issues, but do not hear God's Word or see the beauty of His works. Verse 22 is a

Isaiah 42:1-25

terrifying verse in that we are all referred to as sometimes catching ourselves in our own self-righteousness and hatred, dividing by denomination to justify ourselves instead of seeing honest differences in relationship. While the ending seems a warning, it is also an invitation to come to faith.

Questions to ask:
- Which of the words, lines, or ideas do you recognize from Masonic Work? (Remember to not write them down)
- How do these words, lines, or ideas take the meaning of the degrees and Masonic work and focus them to help make our lives more fit for the Builder's purpose and be Good Men and Masons?
- How do these words, lines, or ideas build our Faith in the Great Architect of the Universe?
- Which of these words, lines, or ideas OTHER than what is used in your Masonic jurisdiction help you to maintain your integrity and work for peace and justice?
- Discuss how these lines could be misunderstood or taken for other purposes that do not glorify God or help you grow as Masons.

NOTES:

Ezekiel 44:1-14

¹Then He brought me back by the way of the outer gate of the sanctuary, which faces the east; and it was shut. ²The LORD said to me, "This gate shall be shut; it shall not be opened, and no one shall enter by it, for the LORD God of Israel has entered by it; therefore it shall be shut. ³"As for the prince, he shall sit in it as prince to eat bread before the LORD; he shall enter by way of the porch of the gate and shall go out by the same way."

⁴Then He brought me by way of the north gate to the front of the house; and I looked, and behold, the glory of the LORD filled the house of the LORD, and I fell on my face. ⁵The LORD said to me, "Son of man, mark well, see with your eyes and hear with your ears all that I say to you concerning all the statutes of the house of the LORD and concerning all its laws; and mark well the entrance of the house, with all exits of the sanctuary. ⁶"You shall say to the rebellious ones, to the house of Israel, 'Thus says the Lord GOD, "Enough of all your abominations, O house of Israel, ⁷when you brought in foreigners, uncircumcised in heart and uncircumcised in flesh, to be in My sanctuary to profane it, even My house, when you offered My food, the fat and the blood; for they made My covenant void—this in addition to all your abominations. ⁸"And you have not kept charge of My holy things yourselves, but you have set foreigners to keep charge of My sanctuary."

⁹"Thus says the Lord GOD, "No foreigner uncircumcised in heart and uncircumcised in flesh, of all the foreigners who are among the sons of Israel, shall enter My sanctuary. ¹⁰"But the Levites who went far from Me when Israel went astray, who went astray from Me after their idols, shall bear the

Ezekiel 44:1-14

punishment for their iniquity. ¹¹"Yet they shall be ministers in My sanctuary, having oversight at the gates of the house and ministering in the house; they shall slaughter the burnt offering and the sacrifice for the people, and they shall stand before them to minister to them. ¹²"Because they ministered to them before their idols and became a stumbling block of iniquity to the house of Israel, therefore I have sworn against them," declares the Lord GOD, "that they shall bear the punishment for their iniquity. ¹³"And they shall not come near to Me to serve as a priest to Me, nor come near to any of My holy things, to the things that are most holy; but they will bear their shame and their abominations which they have committed. ¹⁴"Yet I will appoint them to keep charge of the house, of all its service and of all that shall be done in it.

There are no definitive guides to show us what Solomon's Temple looked like, but rather only written descriptions. The section in 1 Kings 6:31 describes the doors of the inner sanctum of Solomon's Temple as having five *mezuzot* (מזוזות)- the plural form of *mezuzah*). Different translations treat this word differently, from one-fifth of the size of the wall to five door posts, which is how it is most often defined.

The next gate of Solomon's Temple going out had four *mezuzot* (1 Kings 6:33). And the gate to Solomon palace had three of *mezuzot* (1 Kings 7:5) The numbers of doorposts or gates themselves seem to be in sets of 3-4-5 in their descriptions.

Often, we want to think that we see all in front of us, notice all that is there, and understand perfectly what everything means. This passage is reminding us that we do not pay attention to how the Word of God fits into our lives. We try to make it convenient for ourselves. Some

Ezekiel 44:1-14

people teach themselves *eisegeses*[11], which means to read *into* scripture specific ideas that are not there, but allows them to fit it to their own preconceived notions. Properly, scriptural study is through *exegesis*[12], which means reading scripture to understand what God has put into it for us. God is telling us to pay attention here to what scripture says, what it means, and how we are to interact with it.

Questions to ask:
- Which of the words, lines, or ideas do you recognize from Masonic Work? (Remember to not write them down)

---

[11] A comparatively modern term to describe, disapprovingly, a piece of scholarship which appears to find in a given text a significance alien to its context. This might be to provide biblical support for a doctrinal position already held. The term was coined (from the Greek *eis*, in, and *egeisthai*, to guide) as the opposite of exegesis (Greek *ek*), which means an elucidation of. An example of eisegesis is when theologians holding a theory about Christian initiation argued for supporting evidence in the gospels. It was suggested that baptism both effects forgiveness of sins and imparts the gift of the Spirit, but that this rite became split into two parts, i.e. baptism in water soon after birth and the laying on of hands (episcopal confirmation) at a later date but equally essential to the wholeness of the rite. It was suggested that the two parts of the rite were anticipated at the baptism of Jesus: first the baptism in the river (Mark 1: 9), followed as a second constituent of the rite by the descent of the Spirit (Mark 1: 10). (from:
http://www.oxfordbiblicalstudies.com/article/opr/t94/e583?_hi=4&_pos=1)

[12] Defined as a Greek word (found in the **LXX** but not in NT) meaning 'explanation'. It refers nowadays to commentary on the biblical text to elucidate obscurities and to relate one word or verse or section to others in order to define exact meanings. Modern exegesis therefore makes use of textual criticism and linguistic expertise as well as historical and literary disciplines and can also make use of archaeological discoveries. Mistakes in any of these areas could result in false exegesis, as was the case with exegesis of Jesus' parables about the kingdom of God as long as the Kingdom continued to be identified with the Church. (from http://www.oxfordbiblicalstudies.com/article/opr/t94/e644)

Ezekiel 44:1-14

- How do these words, lines, or ideas take the meaning of the degrees and Masonic work and focus them to help make our lives more fit for the Builder's purpose and be Good Men and Masons?
- How do these words, lines, or ideas build our Faith in the Great Architect of the Universe?
- Which of these words, lines, or ideas OTHER than what is used in your Masonic jurisdiction help you to maintain your integrity and work for peace and justice?
- Discuss how these lines could be misunderstood or taken for other purposes that do not glorify God or help you grow as Masons.

NOTES:

Amos 7:1-9

¹ Thus hath the Lord God shewed unto me; and, behold, he formed grasshoppers in the beginning of the shooting up of the latter growth; and, lo, it was the latter growth after the king's mowings. ² And it came to pass, that when they had made an end of eating the grass of the land, then I said, O Lord God, forgive, I beseech thee: by whom shall Jacob arise? for he is small. ³ The Lord repented for this: It shall not be, saith the Lord. ⁴ Thus hath the Lord God shewed unto me: and, behold, the Lord God called to contend by fire, and it devoured the great deep, and did eat up a part. ⁵ Then said I, O Lord God, cease, I beseech thee: by whom shall Jacob arise? for he is small. ⁶ The Lord repented for this: This also shall not be, saith the Lord God. ⁷ Thus he shewed me: and, behold, the Lord stood upon a wall made by a plumbline, with a plumbline in his hand. ⁸ And the Lord said unto me, Amos, what seest thou? And I said, A plumbline. Then said the Lord, Behold, I will set a plumbline in the midst of my people Israel: I will not again pass by them any more: ⁹ And the high places of Isaac shall be desolate, and the sanctuaries of Israel shall be laid waste; and I will rise against the house of Jeroboam with the sword.

The beginning of this section reminds us that Israel has been devastated in many ways during its history. Israel had been a sinful nation and broken their end of God's Covenant during Amos' time. Step by step, however, God tries to bring His people back through lessons of mercy, in spite of how evil and unfaithful the people have been.

Amos 7:1-9

The image of locusts taking all that is left of the grass so that there will be no more good growth for livestock, meaning that people will also starve. When fire burns up all of the roots and remaining grass, famine will be spreading soon. God used these natural forces as His instruments of justice, just as He used the King of Assyria to punish the nation of Israel. The entirety of Israel had been diminished, and there were real questions if God would continue to allow the people to live in heresy and evil.

In verse seven we get to the main point. God threatens Israel with a plumbline. While the plumbline is not a weapon to be feared, it is an indicator of how upright something is. Walls and houses were built with plumblines, but they were also torn down after being measured with a plumbline. If the house was not true and plumb, it should be torn down and a new one built in its place. Similarly, if people are not true and upright, they should not see a lot of mercy. The House of Israel, or any of our houses, should be torn down and new houses put in their place.

Great examples of the plumbline being used as a judgement exist, such as in 2 Kings 21:13, Isaiah 28:17, Isaiah 34:11, and Lamentations 2:8. Each of these is worth reading and seeing how God uses the plumbline to show when people are not upright, and what happens to them.

Luckily for Israel, Amos was a great prophet and prayed for the people of Israel, asking that God might be merciful and not judge them too harshly. God is always merciful and loving, so He only teaches Israel another lesson. This should remind readers of Revelation 9. There, locusts are used to punish and warn, and remind people that it could have been much worse if God was not so very merciful. God could have wiped out Israel in Amos 7, or all of humanity in Revelation 9, but instead He stopped, was merciful and kind, and simply gave a lesson that allowed a lot of people to learn and be saved by His unending grace. Those who sin against God are not worthy of mercy, but

Amos 7:1-9

God so loved the world that He gives many opportunities. Remember that God does not delight in suffering, and does not want the death of a sinner, but that the sinner might be saved.

The question for us today is how we learn from this lesson. In Masonry we are taught to use the builder's tools in an allegorical sense. We consider the uprightness of our lives and try to live more just and noble lives, avoiding selfishness and greed, and trying to measure up to the expectations of our faith and our families and communities.

As Masons, we are to consider our actions and measure ourselves by the Volume of Sacred Law upon our altars. The Bible is that book for most masons, and in its pages we see the errors of our ways of greed and lust, of gluttony and arrogance. Scriptures remind us that we are Fallen and completely dependent upon God's grace. In scripture and older prayers, the word **miserable** is used often.

Many people hate hearing that word, miserable, and get mad when people in the church tell them that they are miserable. This word did not mean wretchedly unhappy or uncomfortable, not did it mean something pitiably small or inadequate. Rather, from the Latin root *miseriae*, meaning in need of mercy, we get another picture.

We are all miserable, as we are all in need of God's mercy. As masons, we recognize that we need the mercy of God, and that we are empowered to do something about our rectitude. We can walk uprightly, doing good and promoting peace and freedom. Every time we right wrongs and fight oppression, we are doing good work, not for its own merit, but as an expression of our faith and love, caused by our faith and love.

In and out of Lodge, we should also help each other in brotherly love by being plumblines for each other, gently and lovingly measuring each other and helping make corrections as we build our lives to be just and upright before God. Our obligations are only the starting points, not the end of the journey. We grow and develop and build

Amos 7:1-9

our lives in honor of God. If we do this well, we will act the way that we are commanded to:

> 8 He has shown you, O mortal, what is good.
>   And what does the Lord require of you?
> To act justly and to love mercy
>   and to walk humbly with your God.
>   -Micah 6:8 (NIV)

Questions to ask:
- Which of the words, lines, or ideas do you recognize from Masonic Work? (Remember to not write them down)
- How do these words, lines, or ideas take the meaning of the degrees and Masonic work and focus them to help make our lives more fit for the Builder's purpose and be Good Men and Masons?
- How do these words, lines, or ideas build our Faith in the Great Architect of the Universe?
- Which of these words, lines, or ideas OTHER than what is used in your Masonic jurisdiction help you to maintain your integrity and work for peace and justice?
- Discuss how these lines could be misunderstood or taken for other purposes that do not glorify God or help you grow as Masons.

Amos 7:1-9

NOTES:

Haggai 1:1-11

¹In the second year of Darius the king, in the sixth month, in the first day of the month, came the word of the LORD by Haggai the prophet unto Zerubbabel the son of Shealtiel, governor of Judah, and to Joshua the son of Josedech, the high priest, saying, ²Thus speaketh the LORD of hosts, saying, This people say, The time is not come, the time that the LORD'S house should be built. ³Then came the word of the LORD by Haggai the prophet, saying, ⁴*Is it* time for you, O ye, to dwell in your cieled houses, and this house *lie* waste? ⁵Now therefore thus saith the LORD of hosts; Consider your ways. ⁶Ye have sown much, and bring in little; ye eat, but ye have not enough; ye drink, but ye are not filled with drink; ye clothe you, but there is none warm; and he that earneth wages earneth wages *to put it* into a bag with holes. ⁷Thus saith the LORD of hosts; Consider your ways. ⁸Go up to the mountain, and bring wood, and build the house; and I will take pleasure in it, and I will be glorified, saith the LORD. ⁹Ye looked for much, and, lo, *it came* to little; and when ye brought *it* home, I did blow upon it. Why? saith the LORD of hosts. Because of mine house that *is* waste, and ye run every man unto his own house. ¹⁰Therefore the heaven over you is stayed from dew, and the earth is stayed *from* her fruit. ¹¹And I called for a drought upon the land, and upon the mountains, and upon the corn, and upon the new wine, and upon the oil, and upon *that* which the ground bringeth forth, and upon men, and upon cattle, and upon all the labour of the hands.

This opening of Haggai puts three important characters in one place: Zerubbabel, Jeshua (Joshua), and

Haggai 1:1-11

Haggai. In Ezra and Nehemiah, Haggai is not present, but there are three roles represented here. First, Zerubbabel, whose name means *"pressed out of Babylon or Babel,"* is the princely ruler whose political oversight is important. Remember that Babel is another name for *"confusion,"* so he was removed from confusion in order to rule Israel and get them into a protected military and political status. Jeshua, whose name means *"salvation,"* is the priestly leader of the people who directs the work and sets up the redevelopment of the places and system of worship. Haggai the prophet's name means *"my festival"* or *"celebration"* prophesizes that the people of Israel will be brought back to full union with God, even after their apostasy and failures. It is important to note that Haggai is not mentioned in the books of Ezra or Nehemiah, where the main stories of Zerubbabel and Jeshua appear.

These three central figures partner together in this book, the shortest in scripture, to bring coming out of confusion back to faith a salvation and deserving of a celebration. God reminds the people of why they had been exiled, and why they need to follow these new leaders back to true faith and worship of the Most High God.

Questions to ask:
- Which of the words, lines, or ideas do you recognize from Masonic Work? (Remember to not write them down)
- How do these words, lines, or ideas take the meaning of the degrees and Masonic work and focus them to help make our lives more fit for the Builder's purpose and be Good Men and Masons?
- How do these words, lines, or ideas build our Faith in the Great Architect of the Universe?
- Which of these words, lines, or ideas OTHER than what is used in your Masonic jurisdiction help you

Haggai 1:1-11

to maintain your integrity and work for peace and justice?
- Discuss how these lines could be misunderstood or taken for other purposes that do not glorify God or help you grow as Masons.

NOTES:

Haggai 2:20-23

[20]And again the word of the LORD came unto Haggai in the four and twentieth day of the month, saying, [21]Speak to Zerubbabel, governor of Judah, saying, I will shake the heavens and the earth; [22]And I will overthrow the throne of kingdoms, and I will destroy the strength of the kingdoms of the heathen; and I will overthrow the chariots, and those that ride in them; and the horses and their riders shall come down, every one by the sword of his brother. [23]In that day, saith the LORD of hosts, will I take thee, O Zerubbabel, my servant, the son of Shealtiel, saith the LORD, and will make thee as a signet: for I have chosen thee, saith the LORD of hosts.

This passage is often looked at only in context of God overthrowing earthly authority that does not follow His commandments. It is a warning that God is the source of all authority and only by Gods will do any humans rule others. What we get wrong so often throughout history is the thought that we have might ourselves, and that we are in charge.

The term 'I will make thee as a signet" is often misunderstood. There did not need to be an actual signet ring that could be worn and shown to people, but a change of heart and being. A signet ring was used to mark official status on documents, whether in wax or clay. Zerubbabel was a person in charge, and he was a man of dignity and honor because of his strong faith and willingness to follow God's commands. Zerubbabel did not forget to thank God for the gifts he was given, whether wisdom or wealth or health.

Haggai 2:20-23

Questions to ask:
- Which of the words, lines, or ideas do you recognize from Masonic Work? (Remember to not write them down)
- How do these words, lines, or ideas take the meaning of the degrees and Masonic work and focus them to help make our lives more fit for the Builder's purpose and be Good Men and Masons?
- How do these words, lines, or ideas build our Faith in the Great Architect of the Universe?
- Which of these words, lines, or ideas OTHER than what is used in your Masonic jurisdiction help you to maintain your integrity and work for peace and justice?
- Discuss how these lines could be misunderstood or taken for other purposes that do not glorify God or help you grow as Masons.

NOTES:

Zechariah 4:1-14

¹And the angel that talked with me came again, and waked me, as a man that is wakened out of his sleep, ²And said unto me, What seest thou? And I said, I have looked, and behold a candlestick all of gold, with a bowl upon the top of it, and his seven lamps thereon, and seven pipes to the seven lamps, which are upon the top thereof: ³And two olive trees by it, one upon the right side of the bowl, and the other upon the left side thereof. ⁴So I answered and spake to the angel that talked with me, saying, What are these, my lord? ⁵Then the angel that talked with me answered and said unto me, Knowest thou not what these be? And I said, No, my lord. ⁶Then he answered and spake unto me, saying, This is the word of the LORD unto Zerubbabel, saying, Not by might, nor by power, but by my spirit, saith the LORD of hosts. ⁷Who art thou, O great mountain? before Zerubbabel thou shalt become a plain: and he shall bring forth the headstone thereof with shoutings, crying, Grace, grace unto it. ⁸Moreover the word of the LORD came unto me, saying, ⁹The hands of Zerubbabel have laid the foundation of this house; his hands shall also finish it; and thou shalt know that the LORD of hosts hath sent me unto you. ¹⁰For who hath despised the day of small things? for they shall rejoice, and shall see the plummet in the hand of Zerubbabel with those seven; they *are* the eyes of the LORD, which run to and fro through the whole earth.
¹¹Then answered I, and said unto him, What are these two olive trees upon the right side of the candlestick and upon the left side thereof? ¹²And I answered again, and said unto him, What be these two olive branches which through the two golden

pipes empty the golden oil out of themselves? [13]And he answered me and said, Knowest thou not what these be? And I said, No, my lord. [14]Then said he, These are the two anointed ones, that stand by the Lord of the whole earth.

This vision is one in a series of visions. In the preceding vision, Jeshua the High Priest was restored in his ability to enter the sanctuary. In this, Zerubbabel, the princely ruler, is shown completing his work of rebuilding the Temple by the light of the Golden Candlestick. The candlestick is a self-feeding light that does not require any assistance from human beings, just as God's Glory does not need any assistance from human beings. The seven pipes indicate the perfection of supply that can only come from God, the two olive trees showing a balance of nature as all other symbols of trees, such as in the Garden of Eden. The Angel speaking is surprised that Zechariah does not understand these things, and that they must be explained to the prophet. Theologically, the key to this passage is in verses 6 and 7, where there is a reminder that it is not human hands that can do anything, but through faith in God. God does all of the real work, we sometimes get the privilege of helping in small ways, like a child might help bake a cake, but really is only licking the spoon. The candlestick image is used again, and for similar purposes, in Revelation 1:20, showing that the lamp for the Jewish people was continued for the Christian church.

The candlestick represents the true office of Israel, and of the Church: to be a light that sends forth its rays into the darkness. Just as Zerubbabel means coming from confusion, all people of faith should be coming forth from darkness and confusion into light through the study and application of scripture to our lives. Because Zerubbabel was faithful, his work holds a plumbline to evaluate the work of others, not as judge, but as example. If we hold our faith, we can accomplish much. This is one of the greatest lessons any man or mason could ever learn.

Questions to ask:
- Which of the words, lines, or ideas do you recognize from Masonic Work? (Remember to not write them down)
- How do these words, lines, or ideas take the meaning of the degrees and Masonic work and focus them to help make our lives more fit for the Builder's purpose and be Good Men and Masons?
- How do these words, lines, or ideas build our Faith in the Great Architect of the Universe?
- Which of these words, lines, or ideas OTHER than what is used in your Masonic jurisdiction help you to maintain your integrity and work for peace and justice?
- Discuss how these lines could be misunderstood or taken for other purposes that do not glorify God or help you grow as Masons.

NOTES:

Apocrypha

1 Esdras 3 to 1 Esdras 4

1 Esdras 3

¹The Emperor Darius gave a great banquet for all those under him, all the members of his family and staff, all the leading officials of Persia and Media, ²all his chief officers, administrators, and the governors of the 127 provinces stretching from India to Ethiopia. ³When everyone had enough to eat and drink, they left, and Darius went to bed. He fell asleep but soon awoke. ⁴Then the three young men who served Emperor Darius as his personal bodyguard said to one another, ⁵"Let each one of us name the one thing that he considers the strongest thing in the world. The emperor will decide who has given the wisest answer to this question and will give magnificent gifts and prizes to the winner. ⁶He will wear royal robes, drink from a gold cup, and sleep in a gold bed. He will have a chariot with gold-studded bridles, wear a fine linen turban, and have a gold necklace. ⁷Because of his wisdom he will be an adviser to the emperor and will be given the title "Relative of the Emperor." ⁸Then each of them wrote down the best answer he could think of, sealed it, and put it under the emperor's pillow. They said to one another, ⁹"When the emperor wakes up, the statements will be given to him. He and the three leading officials of Persia will decide who gave the wisest answer. The winner will be given the prize on the basis of what he has written." ¹⁰The first wrote, "There is nothing stronger than wine." ¹¹The second wrote, "There is nothing

stronger than the emperor." ^{12}And the third wrote, "There is nothing stronger than a woman, but truth can conquer anything." ^{13}When the emperor woke up, the written statements were given to him, and he read them. ^{14}Then he sent messengers and called together all the leading officials of Persia and Media, including the chief officers, administrators, governors, and commissioners. ^{15}He took his seat in the council chamber and had the three statements read aloud. ^{16}"Bring in the three young men," he said, "and let them explain their answers." So when they were brought in, ^{17}they were asked to explain what they had written. The bodyguard who had written about the strength of wine spoke first: ^{18} "Gentlemen," he began, "wine is clearly the strongest thing in the world. It confuses the mind of everyone who drinks it. ^{19}It has exactly the same effect on everyone: king or orphan, slave or free, rich or poor. ^{20}It makes every thought happy and carefree, and makes one forget every sorrow and responsibility. ^{21}It makes everyone feel rich, ignore the power of kings and officials, and talk as if he owned the whole world. ^{22}When men drink wine, they forget who their friends and neighbors are, and then they are soon drawing their swords to fight them. ^{23} Then, when they sober up, they don't remember what they have done. ^{24}Gentlemen," he concluded, "if wine makes men act in this way, it certainly must be the strongest thing in the world."

1 Esdras 4

¹The bodyguard who had written about the strength of the emperor spoke next. ²"Gentlemen," he began, "nothing in the world is stronger than men, since they rule over land and sea and, in fact, over everything in the world. ³But the emperor is the strongest of them all; he is their lord and master, and men obey him, no matter what he commands. ⁴If he tells them to make war on one another, they do it. If he sends them out against his enemies, they go, even if they have to break down mountains, walls, or towers. ⁵They may kill or be killed, but they never disobey the emperor's orders. If they are victorious, they bring him all their loot and everything else they have taken in battle. ⁶Farmers do not go out to war, but even they bring to the emperor a part of everything that they harvest, and they compel one another to pay taxes to the emperor. ⁷Although the emperor is only one man, if he orders people to kill, they kill; if he orders them to set prisoners free, they do it; ⁸if he orders them to attack, they do; if he orders destruction, they destroy; if he orders them to build, they build; ⁹if he orders crops to be destroyed or fields to be planted, it is done. ¹⁰Everybody, soldier or civilian, obeys the emperor. And when he sits down to eat or drink and then falls asleep, ¹¹his servants stand guard around him, without being able to go and take care of their own affairs, for they never disobey him.

¹²Gentlemen," he concluded, "since people obey the emperor like this, certainly nothing in the world is stronger than he is." ¹³The bodyguard who had written about women and the truth - it was Zerubbabel - spoke last. ¹⁴"Gentlemen," he began,

1 Esdras 3 to 1 Esdras 4

"the emperor is certainly powerful, men are numerous, and wine is strong, but who rules and controls them all? It is women! [15] Women gave birth to the emperor and all the men who rule over land and sea. [16] Women brought them into the world. Women brought up the men who planted the vineyards from which wine comes. [17] Women make the clothes that men wear; women bring honor to men; in fact, without women, men couldn't live. [18] "Men may accumulate silver or gold or other beautiful things, but if they see a woman with a pretty face or a good figure, [19] they will leave it all to gape and stare, and they will desire her more than their wealth. [20] A man will leave his own father, who brought him up, and leave his own country to get married. [21] He will forget his father, his mother, and his country to spend the rest of his life with his wife. [22] So you must recognize that women are your masters. Don't you work and sweat and then take all that you have earned and give it to your wives? [23] A man will take his sword and go out to attack, rob and steal, and sail the seas and rivers. [24] He may have to face lions or travel in the dark, but when he has robbed, stolen, and plundered, he will bring the loot home to the woman he loves. [25] "A man loves his wife more than his parents. [26] Some men are driven out of their minds on account of a woman, and others become slaves for the sake of a woman. [27] Others have been put to death, have ruined their lives, or have committed crimes because of a woman. [28] So now do you believe me? "The emperor's power is certainly great - no nation has the courage to attack him. [29] But once I saw him with

Apame, his concubine, the daughter of the famous Bartacus. While sitting at the emperor's right, [30]she took his crown off his head, put it on her own, and then slapped his face with her left hand. [31]All the emperor did was look at her with his mouth open. Whenever she smiles at him, he smiles back; and when she gets angry with him, he flatters her and teases her until she is in a good mood again. [32]Gentlemen, if women can do all that, surely there can be nothing stronger in the world." [33]The emperor and his officials just looked at one another.

Then Zerubbabel began to speak about truth. [34]"Yes, gentlemen," he said, "women are very strong. But think of how big the earth is, how high the sky is; think how fast the sun moves, as it rapidly circles the whole sky in a single day. [35]If the sun can do this, it is certainly great. But truth is greater and stronger than all of these things. [36]Everyone on earth honors truth; heaven praises it; all creation trembles in awe before it. "There is not the slightest injustice in truth. [37]You will find injustice in wine, the emperor, women, all human beings, in all they do, and in everything else. There is no truth in them; they are unjust and they will perish. [38]But truth endures and is always strong; it will continue to live and reign forever. [39]Truth shows no partiality or favoritism; it does what is right, rather than what is unjust or evil. Everyone approves what truth does; [40]its decisions are always fair. Truth is strong, royal, powerful, and majestic forever. Let all things praise the God of truth!" [41]When Zerubbabel had finished speaking, all the people shouted, "Truth is great -

there is nothing stronger!" ⁴²Then the emperor said to him, "You may ask anything you want, even more than what was agreed, and I will give it to you. You will be my adviser, and you will be granted the title "Relative of the Emperor." ⁴³Zerubbabel replied, "Your Majesty, permit me to remind you of the solemn vow you took on the day you became emperor. You promised to rebuild Jerusalem ⁴⁴and to send back all the treasures that had been taken from the city. Remember that when Cyrus made a vow to destroy Babylon, he set these things aside and solemnly promised to send them back to Jerusalem. ⁴⁵You also promised to rebuild the Temple, which the Edomites burned down when the Babylonians devastated the land of Judah. ⁴⁶So, Your Majesty, because you are a man of generosity, I beg you to fulfill the solemn promise you made to the King of heaven." ⁴⁷Then Emperor Darius stood up, kissed Zerubbabel, and wrote letters for him to all the treasurers, governors, and administrators in the provinces, ordering them to provide safe conduct for him and all those going with him to rebuild Jerusalem. ⁴⁸He also wrote letters to all the governors in Greater Syria and Phoenicia, with special instructions to those in Lebanon, to transport cedar logs to Jerusalem and help Zerubbabel rebuild the city. ⁴⁹The emperor also provided letters for all the Jews who wished to return to Jerusalem. These letters guaranteed their freedom and ordered all governors, treasurers, and other administrators not to interfere with them in any way. ⁵⁰All the land that they acquired was to be exempt from taxation, and the Edomites were to

1 Esdras 3 to 1 Esdras 4

surrender the villages they had taken from the Jews. ⁵¹Each year 1,500 pounds of silver would be given for the construction of the Temple until it was finished. ⁵²In addition, 750 pounds of silver would be given each year to provide for the seventeen burnt offerings to be offered in the Temple each day. ⁵³All the Jews who left Babylonia to build the city of Jerusalem would be granted their freedom, together with their children and the priests. ⁵⁴The emperor's orders gave specific instructions, as follows: the priests must be supported, their robes for the Temple service must be provided, ⁵⁵the Levites must be supported until the Temple and Jerusalem are completely rebuilt, ⁵⁶and land and wages must be provided for all the guards of the city. ⁵⁷He also reaffirmed Cyrus' instructions that all the small utensils and Temple treasures that Cyrus had set aside should be returned to Jerusalem. ⁵⁸Then the young man Zerubbabel left the council chamber, turned toward Jerusalem, looked up to heaven, and praised the King of heaven: ⁵⁹"Lord, all praise belongs to you; you are the source of all victory and wisdom, ⁶⁰and I thank you, O Lord of our ancestors, for giving wisdom to me, your servant." ⁶¹Zerubbabel took the emperor's letters and went to Babylon, where he told the other Jews everything that had happened. ⁶²They praised the God of their ancestors because he had made it possible for them ⁶³to go and rebuild Jerusalem and the Temple which bears his name. For seven days they held a joyful celebration, accompanied by music.

Zerubbabel here gives one of the most beautiful discourses on the topic of Truth. Truth is the Word of God, something that Darius did not have more than passing familiarity with. This event marked a change in how well the Jewish people were regarded by their captors during the Exile, and when power started to shift so that the Jews would be released and returned home to Jerusalem.

Zerubbabel is discussing real truth, in Hebrew it is *'emet* (אֱמֶת pronounced eh-MEHT), which starts with the first letter of the alphabet, the middle letter of the word is the middle letter of the alphabet, and the last letter is the last letter of the alphabet. This helps to explain that the truth is all encompassing, and is a reflection of God, who was, and is, and will ever be. Truth is not something that we can change, and relative truth is never the same as Truth given by God. The other two guards are dealing more with relative truth, as is Zerubbabel with his initial discussion of women, but it is a segue into the most important issue that the King does not want to hear, that even the king is a subject of the Most High God. In verse 40, he comes right out and transitions to the God of truth, since he has made the case that God is Truth, and the only truth that matters is God.

Once the king recognizes the truth of Zerubbabel's discourse, notice that truth appears more easily and overcomes the work of bad people who had hidden truth and kept Jerusalem from being rebuilt. Once Darius sees Truth, he dedicates himself to God in ways that mean the most to him, opening his heart and his treasury. Please note how amazing it would have been that an Israelite was so trusted that he was allowed into the king's presence, much less assigned to be a guard of the imperial bedroom. This speaks to the great integrity of Zerubbabel and why he is worthy of emulation.

1 Esdras 3 to 1 Esdras 4

Questions to ask:
- Which of the words, lines, or ideas do you recognize from Masonic Work? (Remember to not write them down)
- How do these words, lines, or ideas take the meaning of the degrees and Masonic work and focus them to help make our lives more fit for the Builder's purpose and be Good Men and Masons?
- How do these words, lines, or ideas build our Faith in the Great Architect of the Universe?
- Which of these words, lines, or ideas OTHER than what is used in your Masonic jurisdiction help you to maintain your integrity and work for peace and justice?
- Discuss how these lines could be misunderstood or taken for other purposes that do not glorify God or help you grow as Masons.

NOTES:

New Testament

1 Esdras 3 to 1 Esdras4

Matthew 5:13-16

> [13] Ye are the salt of the earth: but if the salt have lost his savour, wherewith shall it be salted? it is thenceforth good for nothing, but to be cast out, and to be trodden under foot of men. [14] Ye are the light of the world. A city that is set on an hill cannot be hid. [15] Neither do men light a candle, and put it under a bushel, but on a candlestick; and it giveth light unto all that are in the house. [16] Let your light so shine before men, that they may see your good works, and glorify your Father which is in heaven.

Salt is not always just salt. In the modern world, salt is seen only as a taste enhancement, not as the single most used food preserver in the world. Salt preserves and it cures meat so that it does not go rancid. If you are the salt of the earth, you are a person who helps avoid the putrefying elements of the world from deteriorating the healthy and good parts, even as it is rubbed in a wound, not to inflict pain, but to prevent infection.

One of the beautiful questions is whether salt can ever lose its flavor. Jesus was not implying a drastic change in chemical structure or composition, but rather usefulness. What is the purpose of salt if salt does not do what it is supposed to do? If something is supposed to be salt, but is not good for cleaning and preserving and making better, then use it for what it might be good for, like casting it on the streets so that we don't slip on the ice. Since modern ideas of hygiene were not as prevalent at the time, unusable items like salt would be ordinarily cast into the street as worthless, and it would not matter to most as it would simply dissolve in the next rain and help prevent things growing in between the paving stones (when such existed in the streets of Jerusalem…).

Matthew 5:13-16

In verse 14, we see an allusion to Jerusalem and the other cities of the Jews, all of which were set on hills for protection, and may have been visible during the Sermon on the Mount here. Cities on hills are to be visible and examples, as in Isaiah 2:2 and Micah 4:1, when people will come streaming to the city whose lights can be seen. If Freemasonry is a city on the hill, we are to be visible and show the world how good and wonderful are the precepts of God upon which we are founded. This is why the next injunctions are stated, that our light should not be hidden for our own benefit, but shared with the world. We do not share with others our good works for the sake of works, but to share the glory of God that we have been blessed to see.

An older person who had a great impact on me as a child once showed me verse 15 in a dramatic way: I was asked what happens if you actually place a bushel over a candle. Obviously, it catches on fire if made of wood as the common word used in the Greek here implies. God gives us the light that we have (see Psalm 36:9), and it is to be used for His purposes, whether we want it to be or not. Remember what happened to Jonah when he did not want to preach to the Ninevites? He got swallowed by the fish and then had to go preach to the Ninevites, who immediately converted to the worship of God. Our biases and bigotries of who should hear God's word and see the actions of Masonic teachings will fall before us and tie us down, but they will not stop the Word from being spread.

Questions to ask:

- Which of the words, lines, or ideas do you recognize from Masonic Work? (Remember to not write them down)
- How do these words, lines, or ideas take the meaning of the degrees and Masonic work and focus them to help make our lives more fit for the Builder's purpose and be Good Men and Masons?

Matthew 5:13-16

- How do these words, lines, or ideas build our Faith in the Great Architect of the Universe?
- Which of these words, lines, or ideas OTHER than what is used in your Masonic jurisdiction help you to maintain your integrity and work for peace and justice?
- Discuss how these lines could be misunderstood or taken for other purposes that do not glorify God or help you grow as Masons.

NOTES:

Matthew 6:9-13

> [9] After this manner therefore pray ye:
>> Our Father which art in heaven, Hallowed be thy name.
>> [10] Thy kingdom come, Thy will be done in earth, as it is in heaven.
>> [11] Give us this day our daily bread.
>> [12] And forgive us our debts, as we forgive our debtors.
>> [13] And lead us not into temptation, but deliver us from evil: For thine is the kingdom, and the power, and the glory, for ever. Amen.

This prayer is designed by Jesus to teach us how to pray, breaking down the prayer to several components. First, we recognize to whom we pray: God the Creator in Heaven, whose name is to be glorified. Second, there is a hope that the Kingdom of God will appear on Earth, in whatever form that is to be, where all people worship God fully and there is no sin. In heaven, all attention is focused on worshipping God, and so it should be for all of God's creatures.

Verse 11 reminds us that we are utterly dependent upon God. Mathew 3:3 reminds us that Man shall not live by bread alone, but by every word that proceeds out of the mouth of God. Both our physical and spiritual lives are dependent upon God, and we should be thankful.

One of the hardest parts to understand in many ways is verse 12, where a conditional clause appears to haunt us in the form of the word "as." Verse 10 uses this conditional clause, but that is an obvious use that we are building the Kingdom of God on earth, so it should be like it is in heaven. In verse 12, however, we are asking to be forgiven of the many faults that we have that might be written in the Book of Life. Here Jesus is reminding us that

Matthew 6:9-13

until we can forgive, we cannot be forgiven. The word "as" is reminding us of this in very real terms. We can only be as forgiven as we can forgive. We owe all to God, and we sometimes hope that God will forget all about how much we owe Him and treat us well. Jesus wanted to get us to see that we are made in the image of God, and that as God's image-bearers we must exercise grace and love and show kindness to other people, forgiving what they have done to us that we have not liked.

    A lot of work has been done on translating verse 13, and debates still rage. God does not actively lead people into temptation, but God allows this to be done, whether by ourselves of through other agency, to strengthen our faith. Some translators prefer to translate by intention instead of word-for-word, in which case it is often rendered as "and save us from the time of trouble," which could be now or later in our lives. We do not want to fall victim to the forces of evil and be drawn into sin. At the end of verse 13, we remind ourselves and God that we understand that He is sovereign over all and deserves to be glorified throughout time.

    In Many Lodges, there is confusion when this prayer is said, as so many people will recite the "trespass" version of this text. It is important to make a note of the background of "trespass/trespasses" here. When writing the first Book of Common Prayer in 1549, Archbishop Thomas Cranmer recognized that there were too many disputes over the Lord's Prayer in The Matthian version (above) or the version found in Luke 11:1-13:

> [1] And it came to pass, that, as he was praying in a certain place, when he ceased, one of his disciples said unto him, Lord, teach us to pray, as John also taught his disciples.
> [2] And he said unto them, When ye pray, say,
> > Our Father which art in heaven, Hallowed be thy name.

Matthew 6:9-13

> Thy kingdom come. Thy will be done, as in heaven, so in earth.
> ³ Give us day by day our daily bread.
> ⁴ And forgive us our sins; for we also forgive every one that is indebted to us. And lead us not into temptation; but deliver us from evil.

When we read the Lucan version, we tend to miss that there is no "for thine is the Kingdom…" at the end. In your mind, as you read Luke's version, you probably added that on. The version in Matthew is so strongly ingrained into us, but not as much as the more common version said in so many churches that is a transliteration (getting the meaning of the original Greek text instead of the precise words) of the Bible, not a translation (getting word-for-word from Greek into English).

There arose a question among scholars of Debt versus Sin. Debt was being used by some to say that they did not need to pay off their debts, as God would forgive them of all debts, no matter what they owed to whomever. Sin created a problem, as we can only sin against God, not against man. Since neither of these two versions from the Bible had yet been translated into English (that was still illegal), Cranmer decided to use the word Trespass, as this was more representative of the meaning behind the scripture than either Debt or Sin, and could be less abused by ordinary people. We trespass against each other all of the time, with infractions of omission as well as commission.

Questions to ask:
- Which of the words, lines, or ideas do you recognize from Masonic Work? (Remember to not write them down)
- How do these words, lines, or ideas take the meaning of the degrees and Masonic work and

Matthew 6:9-13

focus them to help make our lives more fit for the Builder's purpose and be Good Men and Masons?
- How do these words, lines, or ideas build our Faith in the Great Architect of the Universe?
- Which of these words, lines, or ideas OTHER than what is used in your Masonic jurisdiction help you to maintain your integrity and work for peace and justice?
- Discuss how these lines could be misunderstood or taken for other purposes that do not glorify God or help you grow as Masons.

NOTES:

Matthew 7:1-14

¹Judge not, that ye be not judged. ²For with what judgment ye judge, ye shall be judged: and with what measure ye mete, it shall be measured to you again. ³And why beholdest thou the mote that is in thy brother's eye, but considerest not the beam that is in thine own eye? ⁴Or how wilt thou say to thy brother, Let me pull out the mote out of thine eye; and, behold, a beam is in thine own eye? ⁵Thou hypocrite, first cast out the beam out of thine own eye; and then shalt thou see clearly to cast out the mote out of thy brother's eye. ⁶Give not that which is holy unto the dogs, neither cast ye your pearls before swine, lest they trample them under their feet, and turn again and rend you. ⁷Ask, and it shall be given you; seek, and ye shall find; knock, and it shall be opened unto you: ⁸For every one that asketh receiveth; and he that seeketh findeth; and to him that knocketh it shall be opened. ⁹Or what man is there of you, whom if his son ask bread, will he give him a stone? ¹⁰Or if he ask a fish, will he give him a serpent? ¹¹If ye then, being evil, know how to give good gifts unto your children, how much more shall your Father which is in heaven give good things to them that ask him? ¹²Therefore all things whatsoever ye would that men should do to you, do ye even so to them: for this is the law and the prophets. ¹³Enter ye in at the strait gate: for wide is the gate, and broad is the way, that leadeth to destruction, and many there be which go in thereat: ¹⁴Because strait is

Matthew 7:1-14

the gate, and narrow is the way, which leadeth unto life, and few there be that find it.

Verses 1-6 are called the "Do Not Judge" passage (parallels in Luke 6:37-42; Romans 14:1-12). In this section we see that it is not our job to replace God as the judge of humanity, it is our job to love and comfort as God loves and comforts us.

Verses 7-12 are known as the "Ask, Seek, Knock" passage (see also Luke 11:5-13). We are not to be passive, sitting around and waiting for God to do things for us, but we must instigate actions of holiness that are spurred on by our faith.

Verses 13-14 are referred to as "The Narrow Gate" passage (see Luke 13:22-30). Too often we do not keep on the path of God, but wander and meander all over the place looking for an easier way than simply going to God in truth and honesty of His love.

Questions to ask:
- Which of the words, lines, or ideas do you recognize from Masonic Work? (Remember to not write them down)
- How do these words, lines, or ideas take the meaning of the degrees and Masonic work and focus them to help make our lives more fit for the Builder's purpose and be Good Men and Masons?

Matthew 7:1-14

- How do these words, lines, or ideas build our Faith in the Great Architect of the Universe?
- Which of these words, lines, or ideas OTHER than what is used in your Masonic jurisdiction help you to maintain your integrity and work for peace and justice?
- Discuss how these lines could be misunderstood or taken for other purposes that do not glorify God or help you grow as Masons.

NOTES:

Matthew 18:15-20

¹⁵If your brother sins against you, go and confront him privately. If he listens to you, you have won your brother over. ¹⁶But if he will not listen, take one or two others along, so that 'every matter may be established by the testimony of two or three witnesses.' ¹⁷If he refuses to listen to them, tell it to the church. And if he refuses to listen even to the church, regard him as you would a pagan or a tax collector.
¹⁸Truly I tell you, whatever you bind on earth will be bound in heaven, and whatever you loose on earth will be loosed in heaven.
¹⁹Again, I tell you truly that if two of you on the earth agree about anything you ask for, it will be done for you by My Father in heaven. ²⁰For where two or three gather together in My name, there am I with them."

Masons, just like any Christians, are supposed to get along as members of God's family. Unfortunately, brotherly love does not always prevail, and sometimes disputes break out among humans. We are supposed to deal honestly and listen to one another. We are supposed to listen to understand each other, not simply listen to respond to one another and tell of how great we are. We are going to have misunderstandings, but how we fix division is how close to God we are, by the quality of the fruit of our actions. Consider Matthew 7:15-20:

> ¹⁵ Beware of false prophets, which come to you in sheep's clothing, but inwardly they are ravening wolves. ¹⁶ Ye shall know them by their fruits. Do men gather grapes of

Matthew 18:15-20

> thorns, or figs of thistles? [17] Even so every good tree bringeth forth good fruit; but a corrupt tree bringeth forth evil fruit. [18] A good tree cannot bring forth evil fruit, neither can a corrupt tree bring forth good fruit. [19] Every tree that bringeth not forth good fruit is hewn down, and cast into the fire. [20] Wherefore by their fruits ye shall know them.

Verse 16 invokes the injunction from Deuteronomy 19:15-21 to take witnesses with you to settle a dispute so that people can lend counsel and offer assistance. In Lodge, we are to get along, and if we cannot, we resolve it outside of Lodge to provide harmony in the Lodge. We cannot, however, leave disputes unsettled, but rather have to face them and resolve the issue. We resolve things through peace and love, however seeing all sides of an argument. There is never room for the "he said… she said" view of life. Disputes are only settled by discussion and humility. Jesus adds an amusing comment here in verse 17: treat the person as a tax collector and pagan. If you have ever read the New Testament, you know how Jesus always treated pagans and tax collectors: he loved them and treated them with respect and taught them the Gospel. When we have an argument with a brother, we too should treat them with love and respect, showing that we are followers of God, not arrogant believers of self-only.

What we do to each other and how we treat each other matters. If we do not treat others with respect and love, we have not listened to our own words in Lodge, much less the lessons of the Gospel.

Matthew 18:18 is almost word for word the same as what Jesus told Peter in Matthew 16:19, that what you bind on earth is bound in heaven an what is loosed on earth is loosed in heaven. How to interpret these words has been a question for scholars and theologians for 2000 years. The word "bind" (δήσητε) is in a form called the aorist

Matthew 18:15-20

subjunctive active tense, which means that it is a definite idea that what you do will happen and is already set to happen. This is an assurance that your binding or tying will take and not be accidentally set free. If we take 18 and 19 together, there is a different possibility of the meaning here for us. What we bind of our own passions might also appear before us in heaven, and what we let loose might stand to accuse us. When we are together, and we are righteous, and focused on God, we will do God's will rather than simply trying to impose our will on the world. This gets back to the question of people knowing us by our fruits, as in Matthew 7:15-20.

Questions to ask:
- Which of the words, lines, or ideas do you recognize from Masonic Work? (Remember to not write them down)
- How do these words, lines, or ideas take the meaning of the degrees and Masonic work and focus them to help make our lives more fit for the Builder's purpose and be Good Men and Masons?
- How do these words, lines, or ideas build our Faith in the Great Architect of the Universe?
- Which of these words, lines, or ideas OTHER than what is used in your Masonic jurisdiction help you to maintain your integrity and work for peace and justice?
- Discuss how these lines could be misunderstood or taken for other purposes that do not glorify God or help you grow as Masons.

Matthew 18:15-20
NOTES:

Matthew 20:1-16

¹ For the kingdom of heaven is like unto a man that is an householder, which went out early in the morning to hire labourers into his vineyard. ² And when he had agreed with the labourers for a penny a day, he sent them into his vineyard. ³ And he went out about the third hour, and saw others standing idle in the marketplace, ⁴ And said unto them; Go ye also into the vineyard, and whatsoever is right I will give you. And they went their way. ⁵ Again he went out about the sixth and ninth hour, and did likewise. ⁶ And about the eleventh hour he went out, and found others standing idle, and saith unto them, Why stand ye here all the day idle? ⁷ They say unto him, Because no man hath hired us. He saith unto them, Go ye also into the vineyard; and whatsoever is right, that shall ye receive. ⁸ So when even was come, the lord of the vineyard saith unto his steward, Call the labourers, and give them their hire, beginning from the last unto the first. ⁹ And when they came that were hired about the eleventh hour, they received every man a penny. ¹⁰ But when the first came, they supposed that they should have received more; and they likewise received every man a penny. ¹¹ And when they had received it, they murmured against the goodman of the house, ¹² Saying, These last have wrought but one hour, and thou hast made them equal unto us, which have borne the burden and heat of the day. ¹³ But he answered one of them, and said, Friend, I do thee no wrong: didst not thou agree with me for a penny? ¹⁴ Take that thine is, and go thy way: I will give unto this last, even as unto thee. ¹⁵ Is it not lawful for me to do what I will with mine own? Is thine eye evil, because I am good? ¹⁶ So the last shall

Matthew 20:1-16
> be first, and the first last: for many be called, but few chosen.

    Most people read this story and think of the economic ideas of fairness. We live in an ear of concentrated focus on money, the god that most people really worship. If we break the ideas presented here down, we are exploring merit and faithfulness to the work.

    Is it really fair to ask someone to work all day and receive only the same amount as those who have only worked an hour or so? Well, to some this is simply supply and demand: you need the job done, so adding more labor at the end costs more than hiring them up front. The simple economic reality is that a contract is a contract, and the laborers contracted for a set amount and other contractors just got lucky with a generous boss.

    This idea of generosity gets closer to the real issue. God is generous and kind, but this story is not about money. The story is about salvation. Those of us who are from good and faithful households are in no better position for heaven than anyone else who believes, as salvation is by faith alone, irrespective of religious tradition. Most people think of the statement as associated with Martin Luther and his *95 Theses* of 1517, but this same idea is one of Mosaic origin. Belief in God is what makes people want to follow the Law and be set free. The Law does not constrain our faith, it helps develop it further. Luther recognized the writings of the Early Church Fathers, who had read the writings of the rabbis (called Midrash), and saw the truth of faith being the essential element in salvation. Who sets the wags of sin? Who sets the wages of faith? Would you rather be the least in heaven or the first in Hell? There is incredible generosity in God's chancery that someone who has been evil their whole lives might find salvation in faith right before the end. This is the whole point of one of the most important, yet most overlooked verses in the Bible, John 3:17.

Matthew 20:1-16

Most people, even non-Christians, know John 3:16, but they miss the point that it is half of an idea. If we leave out John 3:17, the idea of John 3:16 becomes weaponized; it is used as a threat instead of an invitation and an assurance. In Matthew 20, we are supposed to be able to see the beautiful assurance that no matter how late in the game we come to faith, we still get to enter the gates of heaven if we truly accept God into our hearts.

Questions to ask:
- Which of the words, lines, or ideas do you recognize from Masonic Work? (Remember to not write them down)
- How do these words, lines, or ideas take the meaning of the degrees and Masonic work and focus them to help make our lives more fit for the Builder's purpose and be Good Men and Masons?
- How do these words, lines, or ideas build our Faith in the Great Architect of the Universe?
- Which of these words, lines, or ideas OTHER than what is used in your Masonic jurisdiction help you to maintain your integrity and work for peace and justice?
- Discuss how these lines could be misunderstood or taken for other purposes that do not glorify God or help you grow as Masons.

Matthew 20:1-16
NOTES:

Matthew 25:21

²¹ His lord said unto him, Well done, thou good and faithful servant: thou hast been faithful over a few things, I will make thee ruler over many things: enter thou into the joy of thy lord.

Let's Look at this in Context:

¹⁴ For the kingdom of heaven is as a man travelling into a far country, who called his own servants, and delivered unto them his goods. ¹⁵ And unto one he gave five talents, to another two, and to another one; to every man according to his several ability; and straightway took his journey. ¹⁶ Then he that had received the five talents went and traded with the same, and made them other five talents. ¹⁷ And likewise he that had received two, he also gained other two. ¹⁸ But he that had received one went and digged in the earth, and hid his lord's money. ¹⁹ After a long time the lord of those servants cometh, and reckoneth with them. ²⁰ And so he that had received five talents came and brought other five talents, saying, Lord, thou deliveredst unto me five talents: behold, I have gained beside them five talents more. ²¹ His lord said unto him, Well done, thou good and faithful servant: thou hast been faithful over a few things, I will make thee ruler over many things: enter thou into the joy of thy lord. ²² He also that had received two talents came and said, Lord, thou deliveredst unto me two talents: behold, I have gained two other talents beside them. ²³ His lord said unto him, Well done, good and faithful servant; thou hast been faithful over a few things, I will make thee ruler over many things: enter thou into the joy of thy lord. ²⁴ Then he which had received

Matthew 25:21

the one talent came and said, Lord, I knew thee that thou art an hard man, reaping where thou hast not sown, and gathering where thou hast not strawed: ²⁵ And I was afraid, and went and hid thy talent in the earth: lo, there thou hast that is thine. ²⁶ His lord answered and said unto him, Thou wicked and slothful servant, thou knewest that I reap where I sowed not, and gather where I have not strawed: ²⁷ Thou oughtest therefore to have put my money to the exchangers, and then at my coming I should have received mine own with usury. ²⁸ Take therefore the talent from him, and give it unto him which hath ten talents. ²⁹ For unto every one that hath shall be given, and he shall have abundance: but from him that hath not shall be taken away even that which he hath. ³⁰ And cast ye the unprofitable servant into outer darkness: there shall be weeping and gnashing of teeth. ³¹ When the Son of man shall come in his glory, and all the holy angels with him, then shall he sit upon the throne of his glory: ³² And before him shall be gathered all nations: and he shall separate them one from another, as a shepherd divideth his sheep from the goats: ³³ And he shall set the sheep on his right hand, but the goats on the left. ³⁴ Then shall the King say unto them on his right hand, Come, ye blessed of my Father, inherit the kingdom prepared for you from the foundation of the world: ³⁵ For I was an hungred, and ye gave me meat: I was thirsty, and ye gave me drink: I was a stranger, and ye took me in: ³⁶ Naked, and ye clothed me: I was sick, and ye visited me: I was in prison, and ye came unto me. ³⁷ Then shall the righteous answer him, saying, Lord, when saw we thee an hungred, and fed thee? or thirsty, and gave thee drink? ³⁸ When saw we thee a stranger, and took thee in? or naked, and clothed thee? ³⁹ Or when saw we thee sick, or in prison, and came unto thee? ⁴⁰ And the King shall answer and say unto them, Verily I

Matthew 25:21

say unto you, Inasmuch as ye have done it unto one of the least of these my brethren, ye have done it unto me. [41] Then shall he say also unto them on the left hand, Depart from me, ye cursed, into everlasting fire, prepared for the devil and his angels: [42] For I was an hungred, and ye gave me no meat: I was thirsty, and ye gave me no drink: [43] I was a stranger, and ye took me not in: naked, and ye clothed me not: sick, and in prison, and ye visited me not. [44] Then shall they also answer him, saying, Lord, when saw we thee an hungred, or athirst, or a stranger, or naked, or sick, or in prison, and did not minister unto thee? [45] Then shall he answer them, saying, Verily I say unto you, Inasmuch as ye did it not to one of the least of these, ye did it not to me. [46] And these shall go away into everlasting punishment: but the righteous into life eternal.

This verse has a few words that are almost impossible to translate, as we do not have the concepts in English. The term Well done (Εὖ in Greek), for example, does not translate the force of intent here. This is the verbal equivalent of a standing ovation. A master of slaves would rarely say such a forceful thing, so this was a radical idea that God would be this enthusiastic about humanity doing anything. This was a message of deep relationship that even Israel was not used to.

The term "enter into the joy of thy Lord" was also a set of words too strong for the fit of this parable, as it was unimaginable that any servant could be welcomed into the house of his master as if a full and beloved member of the family. This is the fullness of heaven that God is promising. This brings the rest of the parable into perspective, especially the ending where Jesus is telling us that it is the accumulation of our actions that represent the fruits of our hearts. If our hearts are pure, our actions will be loving and

Matthew 25:21

kind, but sometimes our actions are only seemingly loving or kind, but for ulterior motives. God sees the truth of what we intend as what we are doing.

Questions to ask:
- Which of the words, lines, or ideas do you recognize from Masonic Work? (Remember to not write them down)
- How do these words, lines, or ideas take the meaning of the degrees and Masonic work and focus them to help make our lives more fit for the Builder's purpose and be Good Men and Masons?
- How do these words, lines, or ideas build our Faith in the Great Architect of the Universe?
- Which of these words, lines, or ideas OTHER than what is used in your Masonic jurisdiction help you to maintain your integrity and work for peace and justice?
- Discuss how these lines could be misunderstood or taken for other purposes that do not glorify God or help you grow as Masons.

NOTES:

Matthew 28:1-20

¹In the end of the sabbath, as it began to dawn toward the first day of the week, came Mary Magdalene and the other Mary to see the sepulchre. ² And, behold, there was a great earthquake: for the angel of the Lord descended from heaven, and came and rolled back the stone from the door, and sat upon it. ³ His countenance was like lightning, and his raiment white as snow: ⁴ And for fear of him the keepers did shake, and became as dead men. ⁵ And the angel answered and said unto the women, Fear not ye: for I know that ye seek Jesus, which was crucified. ⁶ He is not here: for he is risen, as he said. Come, see the place where the Lord lay. ⁷ And go quickly, and tell his disciples that he is risen from the dead; and, behold, he goeth before you into Galilee; there shall ye see him: lo, I have told you. ⁸ And they departed quickly from the sepulchre with fear and great joy; and did run to bring his disciples word. ⁹ And as they went to tell his disciples, behold, Jesus met them, saying, All hail. And they came and held him by the feet, and worshipped him. ¹⁰ Then said Jesus unto them, Be not afraid: go tell my brethren that they go into Galilee, and there shall they see me. ¹¹ Now when they were going, behold, some of the watch came into the city, and shewed unto the chief priests all the things that were done. ¹² And when they were assembled with the elders, and had taken counsel, they gave large money unto the soldiers, ¹³ Saying, Say ye, His disciples came by night, and stole him away while we slept. ¹⁴ And if this come to the governor's ears, we will persuade him, and secure you. ¹⁵ So they took the money, and did as they were taught: and this saying is commonly reported among the Jews until this day. ¹⁶ Then the eleven disciples went away into Galilee, into a

Matthew 28:1-20

> mountain where Jesus had appointed them. [17] And when they saw him, they worshipped him: but some doubted. [18] And Jesus came and spake unto them, saying, All power is given unto me in heaven and in earth. [19] Go ye therefore, and teach all nations, baptizing them in the name of the Father, and of the Son, and of the Holy Ghost: [20] Teaching them to observe all things whatsoever I have commanded you: and, lo, I am with you always, even unto the end of the world. Amen.

At first glance, this section might appear to be only of interest to Christians. It recounts the resurrection of Jesus, who died on a cross on Friday afternoon and arose early on Sunday morning. Sunday has always been the beginning of the week, even if Christians celebrate it as the Sabbath in memory of the event in this passage.

For many of us, the idea here is to spread the love. If we get down to it, what are the most important lessons that all people in all ages should learn from Jesus? Jews honor Jesus as a great prophet. Muslims say that Jesus was one of the greatest prophets, and devote more of the Quran to Jesus than to Mohammad. Jesus often summed the law in orthodox Hebrew terms, as when he quotes Deuteronomy 6:4-7 (NKJV)

> [4] "Hear, O Israel: The Lord our God, the Lord is one! [5] You shall love the Lord your God with all your heart, with all your soul, and with all your strength. [6] "And these words which I command you today shall be in your heart. [7] You shall teach them diligently to your children, and shall talk of them

when you sit in your house, when you walk by the way, when you lie down, and when you rise up.

Jesus repeats these words in Matthew 22:37-40, Mark 12:30-31, and Luke 10:27, and adds to them the second element of Leviticus 19:9-18, which deals with loving neighbors in examples from the Ten Commandments and beyond. In that passage, verse 18 states carefully that "you shall love your neighbor as yourself: I am the Lord." Apparently the disciples and followers did not take these injunctions to heart enough to act on them, so Jesus states it again in his own way:

> [34] A new commandment I give unto you, That ye love one another; as I have loved you, that ye also love one another. [35] By this shall all men know that ye are my disciples, if ye have love one to another. John 13:34-35 (KJV)

Some might find the relationship easier to see in other translations of scripture:

> [34] "A new command I give you: Love one another. As I have loved you, so you must love one another. [35] By this everyone will know that you are my disciples, if you love one another." (NIV)

The principle issue of this passage is that God is the God of Love, and that love conquers all, even death. If we are to be true Masons, we must learn to love, and to build our lives on foundations of love, or else we will build on the shifting sands of fear instead.

Questions to ask:

Matthew 28:1-20

- Which of the words, lines, or ideas do you recognize from Masonic Work? (Remember to not write them down)
- How do these words, lines, or ideas take the meaning of the degrees and Masonic work and focus them to help make our lives more fit for the Builder's purpose and be Good Men and Masons?
- How do these words, lines, or ideas build our Faith in the Great Architect of the Universe?
- Which of these words, lines, or ideas OTHER than what is used in your Masonic jurisdiction help you to maintain your integrity and work for peace and justice?
- Discuss how these lines could be misunderstood or taken for other purposes that do not glorify God or help you grow as Masons.

NOTES:

John 19:1-42

[1] Then Pilate therefore took Jesus, and scourged him. [2] And the soldiers platted a crown of thorns, and put it on his head, and they put on him a purple robe, [3] And said, Hail, King of the Jews! and they smote him with their hands. [4] Pilate therefore went forth again, and saith unto them, Behold, I bring him forth to you, that ye may know that I find no fault in him. [5] Then came Jesus forth, wearing the crown of thorns, and the purple robe. And Pilate saith unto them, Behold the man! [6] When the chief priests therefore and officers saw him, they cried out, saying, Crucify him, crucify him. Pilate saith unto them, Take ye him, and crucify him: for I find no fault in him. [7] The Jews answered him, We have a law, and by our law he ought to die, because he made himself the Son of God. [8] When Pilate therefore heard that saying, he was the more afraid; [9] And went again into the judgment hall, and saith unto Jesus, Whence art thou? But Jesus gave him no answer. [10] Then saith Pilate unto him, Speakest thou not unto me? knowest thou not that I have power to crucify thee, and have power to release thee? [11] Jesus answered, Thou couldest have no power at all against me, except it were given thee from above: therefore he that delivered me unto thee hath the greater sin. [12] And from thenceforth Pilate sought to release him: but the Jews cried out, saying, If thou let this man go, thou art not Caesar's friend: whosoever maketh himself a king speaketh against Caesar. [13] When Pilate therefore heard that saying, he brought Jesus forth, and sat down in the judgment seat in a place that is called the Pavement, but in the Hebrew, Gabbatha. [14] And it was the preparation of the passover, and about the sixth hour: and he saith unto the Jews, Behold your King! [15] But they cried

John 19:1-42

out, Away with him, away with him, crucify him. Pilate saith unto them, Shall I crucify your King? The chief priests answered, We have no king but Caesar. [16] Then delivered he him therefore unto them to be crucified. And they took Jesus, and led him away. [17] And he bearing his cross went forth into a place called the place of a skull, which is called in the Hebrew Golgotha: [18] Where they crucified him, and two other with him, on either side one, and Jesus in the midst. [19] And Pilate wrote a title, and put it on the cross. And the writing was JESUS OF NAZARETH THE KING OF THE JEWS. [20] This title then read many of the Jews: for the place where Jesus was crucified was nigh to the city: and it was written in Hebrew, and Greek, and Latin. [21] Then said the chief priests of the Jews to Pilate, Write not, The King of the Jews; but that he said, I am King of the Jews. [22] Pilate answered, What I have written I have written. [23] Then the soldiers, when they had crucified Jesus, took his garments, and made four parts, to every soldier a part; and also his coat: now the coat was without seam, woven from the top throughout. [24] They said therefore among themselves, Let us not rend it, but cast lots for it, whose it shall be: that the scripture might be fulfilled, which saith, They parted my raiment among them, and for my vesture they did cast lots. These things therefore the soldiers did. [25] Now there stood by the cross of Jesus his mother, and his mother's sister, Mary the wife of Cleophas, and Mary Magdalene. [26] When Jesus therefore saw his mother, and the disciple standing by, whom he loved, he saith unto his mother, Woman, behold thy son! [27] Then saith he to the disciple, Behold thy mother! And from that hour that disciple took her unto his own home. [28] After this, Jesus knowing that all things were now accomplished, that the scripture might be fulfilled, saith, I thirst. [29] Now there was set a vessel full of vinegar: and they filled a spunge with vinegar, and put it upon hyssop, and put it to his mouth. ³⁰ When Jesus therefore had received the vinegar, he said, It is finished: and he bowed his head, and gave up the ghost. ³¹ The Jews therefore, because it was the preparation, that the bodies should not remain upon the cross on the sabbath day, (for that sabbath day was an high day,) besought Pilate that their legs might be broken, and that they might be taken away. ³² Then came the soldiers, and brake the legs of the first, and of the other which was crucified with him. ³³ But when they came to Jesus, and saw that he was dead already, they brake not his legs: ³⁴ But one of the soldiers with a spear pierced his side, and forthwith came there out blood and water. ³⁵ And he that saw it bare record, and his record is true: and he knoweth that he saith true, that ye might believe. ³⁶ For these things were done, that the scripture should be fulfilled, A bone of him shall not be broken. ³⁷ And again another scripture saith, They shall look on him whom they pierced. ³⁸ And after this Joseph of Arimathaea, being a disciple of Jesus, but secretly for fear of the Jews, besought Pilate that he might take away the body of Jesus: and Pilate gave him leave. He came therefore, and took the body of Jesus. ³⁹ And there came also Nicodemus, which at the first came to Jesus by night, and brought a mixture of myrrh and aloes, about an hundred pound weight. ⁴⁰ Then took they the body of Jesus, and wound it in linen clothes with the spices, as the manner of the Jews is to bury. ⁴¹ Now in the place where he was crucified there was a garden; and in the garden a new sepulchre, wherein was never man yet laid. ⁴² There laid they Jesus therefore because of the Jews' preparation day; for the sepulchre was nigh at hand.

John 19:1-42

Verses 26 and 27 are often overlooked in the important significance of what has just happened: Jesus performed an adoption. John is now Mary's son, and John will need to take care of her in her old age. Christianity is a religion of adoption, in which we are adopted into the household of God through faith. Remember that at the beginning of Jesus' earthly life he was adopted by Joseph. We hear of God adopting us in numerous passages. What is a fraternity but an adoptive set of brothers who are to love and care for one another?

The very idea of kingship is called into question here. Pilate had earlier asked Jesus the Question of "What is truth" (John 18:38), and his insistence on writing "***King of the Jews***" above Jesus was a rebuke to Israel that it did not see Truth, but saw what they wanted to keep themselves comfortable and in a condition that they understood with relationship to power. The rest of the passage here helps to reinforce this basic question of what is truth, and that the answer is God is Truth, and Christ is the Son of God. *(See comments in 1 Esdras 3-4 above).*

Questions to ask:

- Which of the words, lines, or ideas do you recognize from Masonic Work? (Remember to not write them down)
- How do these words, lines, or ideas take the meaning of the degrees and Masonic work and focus them to help make our lives more fit for the Builder's purpose and be Good Men and Masons?
- How do these words, lines, or ideas build our Faith in the Great Architect of the Universe?
- Which of these words, lines, or ideas OTHER than what is used in your Masonic jurisdiction help you

John 19:1-42

to maintain your integrity and work for peace and justice?
- Discuss how these lines could be misunderstood or taken for other purposes that do not glorify God or help you grow as Masons.

NOTES:

1 Corinthians 6:1-11

¹Does any one of you, when he has a case against his neighbor, dare to go to law before the unrighteous and not before the saints? ²Or do you not know that the saints will judge the world? If the world is judged by you, are you not competent to constitute the smallest law courts? ³Do you not know that we will judge angels? How much more matters of this life? ⁴So if you have law courts dealing with matters of this life, do you appoint them as judges who are of no account in the church? ⁵I say this to your shame. Is it so, that there is not among you one wise man who will be able to decide between his brethren, ⁶but brother goes to law with brother, and that before unbelievers? ⁷Actually, then, it is already a defeat for you, that you have lawsuits with one another. Why not rather be wronged? Why not rather be defrauded? ⁸On the contrary, you yourselves wrong and defraud. You do this even to your brethren. ⁹Or do you not know that the unrighteous will not inherit the kingdom of God? Do not be deceived; neither fornicators, nor idolaters, nor adulterers, nor effeminate, nor homosexuals, ¹⁰nor thieves, nor the covetous, nor drunkards, nor revilers, nor swindlers, will inherit the kingdom of God. ¹¹Such were some of you; but you were washed, but you were sanctified, but you were justified in the name of the Lord Jesus Christ and in the Spirit of our God.

How do we deal with one another? Is there compassion in our hearts? Is there brotherly love from one creature made in the image of God towards another of the same? This rebuke by St. Paul was not only for those who would judge outside of the early church (judging gentiles),

1 Corinthians 6:1-11

but those within the church (even while still in the synagogues). The term "dare" is used with effect here, such that people ask if the person who does dare to do such things has so little regard for the glory of God and the credit of the faith. Why do people sue one another or cause such social difficulties? Jealousy, power, envy, greed? There are lists given in this passage that cover these and beyond.

In a church, or in a Lodge, there should be more compassion and consideration as all of us within either structure recognize that we need Salvation, and we need the grace of one another as well as of God in order to grow and develop into a person who can truly love God wholly. We must bolster each other's faith, not chip away at someone for a perceived slight. If we open ourselves to Truth, then we are to carefully explore our own conscience and work with those who we may have perceived some slight or injustice, and seek understanding before we seek compensation or retribution. Paul is telling us to seek prayerful healing. This is where we must listen to one another, not simply to respond and share our side of the story, but to understand the other person's perspectives. In counseling classes, you are taught that there are two ways of understanding: to respond or to understand. You are also taught that there are always at least three sides to any argument between two people, and this might not even get to questions of what is truth. Seeking truth is difficult, but doing it with charity and humility is the sign of a real mason.

Questions to ask:
- Which of the words, lines, or ideas do you recognize from Masonic Work? (Remember to not write them down)
- How do these words, lines, or ideas take the meaning of the degrees and Masonic work and focus them to help make our lives more fit for the Builder's purpose and be Good Men and Masons?

1 Corinthians 6:1-11
- How do these words, lines, or ideas build our Faith in the Great Architect of the Universe?
- Which of these words, lines, or ideas OTHER than what is used in your Masonic jurisdiction help you to maintain your integrity and work for peace and justice?
- Discuss how these lines could be misunderstood or taken for other purposes that do not glorify God or help you grow as Masons.

NOTES:

1 Corinthians 13:1-13

¹Though I speak with the tongues of men and of angels, and have not charity, I am become as sounding brass, or a tinkling cymbal. ² And though I have the gift of prophecy, and understand all mysteries, and all knowledge; and though I have all faith, so that I could remove mountains, and have not charity, I am nothing. ³ And though I bestow all my goods to feed the poor, and though I give my body to be burned, and have not charity, it profiteth me nothing. ⁴ Charity suffereth long, and is kind; charity envieth not; charity vaunteth not itself, is not puffed up, ⁵ Doth not behave itself unseemly, seeketh not her own, is not easily provoked, thinketh no evil; ⁶ Rejoiceth not in iniquity, but rejoiceth in the truth; ⁷ Beareth all things, believeth all things, hopeth all things, endureth all things. ⁸ Charity never faileth: but whether there be prophecies, they shall fail; whether there be tongues, they shall cease; whether there be knowledge, it shall vanish away. ⁹ For we know in part, and we prophesy in part. ¹⁰ But when that which is perfect is come, then that which is in part shall be done away. ¹¹ When I was a child, I spake as a child, I understood as a child, I thought as a child: but when I became a man, I put away childish things. ¹² For now we see through a glass, darkly; but then face to face: now I know in part; but then shall I know even as also I am known. ¹³ And now abideth faith, hope, charity, these three; but the greatest of these is charity.

While this chapter is often, unfortunately used at weddings because of the beauty of the words, it is not about romantic love. In the KJV, the word agape does mean love, but love of fellow, of friend, and of family. There are several

1 Corinthians 13:1-13

Greek words for Love that are important here: *Eros*, or passionate/romantic love; *Philia*, which is friendship love, and its relative *Philautia*, which is healthy self-love (opposed to hubris); *Storge*, or familial love; *Ludus*, which is playful/flirtatious/kidding love; *Pragma*, which is compatibility and utility; *Agape*, love for everyone. *Agape* (ἀγάπην) was translated by St. Jerome in the Vulgate (First edition of the Bible in Latin in the 380s- remember that Latin was the common language of most people in the Roman Empire, which is why it was used) as *caritas*, which means love for all or charity.

    This passage, in context as opposed to using it at a wedding, is admonishing members of a church who are not getting along to try harder to get along and be civil towards one another. It is an attempt to fix a very broken, very human set of people in their relationships. How many times have you heard in Lodge about the quest for truth, and the essential reality that truth comes only from God? The image that we grow up and put away childish things is essentially talking about the egocentric nature of children, and how as children we do not think of others as we should.

    One of the images that deserves to be discussed further here is that appearing in verse 4, where we are told not to be puffed up with pride. The word here is *physioutai* (φυσιοῦται), which is not puffed up with air in the chest, but puffed up as a carcass on the side of the road, bloated and stinking, filled with sickness and decay. This is what too much pride puts into us- death of relationship and focus only on the self. This is why so many do not mind the translation of agape to Charity, as the love for others needs to be expressed. Christ told us in Matthew 22:21 that we are made in the image of God, yet asked whose image is on the money they pay tribute to Rome with: "They say unto him, Caesar's. Then saith he unto them, Render therefore unto Caesar the things which are Caesar's; and unto God the things that are God's." You are made in God's image, so you are to give God that which is made in His image,

2 Corinthians 5:1-10

or wealth when we stand naked and alone before the great white throne as portrayed in Revelation 20:11. This is essential that we conduct our lives by faith in God, not distracted by the sights of the world around us that detract our attention from the issues that really matter, foremost of which is God's Love and Grace.

Questions to ask:
- Which of the words, lines, or ideas do you recognize from Masonic Work? (Remember to not write them down)
- How do these words, lines, or ideas take the meaning of the degrees and Masonic work and focus them to help make our lives more fit for the Builder's purpose and be Good Men and Masons?
- How do these words, lines, or ideas build our Faith in the Great Architect of the Universe?
- Which of these words, lines, or ideas OTHER than what is used in your Masonic jurisdiction help you to maintain your integrity and work for peace and justice?
- Discuss how these lines could be misunderstood or taken for other purposes that do not glorify God or help you grow as Masons.

2 Corinthians 5:1-10
NOTES:

2 Thessalonians 3:6-16

⁶ Now we command you, brethren, in the name of our Lord Jesus Christ, that ye withdraw yourselves from every brother that walketh disorderly, and not after the tradition which he received of us. ⁷ For yourselves know how ye ought to follow us: for we behaved not ourselves disorderly among you; ⁸ Neither did we eat any man's bread for nought; but wrought with labour and travail night and day, that we might not be chargeable to any of you: ⁹ Not because we have not power, but to make ourselves an ensample unto you to follow us. ¹⁰ For even when we were with you, this we commanded you, that if any would not work, neither should he eat. ¹¹ For we hear that there are some which walk among you disorderly, working not at all, but are busybodies. ¹² Now them that are such we command and exhort by our Lord Jesus Christ, that with quietness they work, and eat their own bread. ¹³ But ye, brethren, be not weary in well doing. ¹⁴ And if any man obey not our word by this epistle, note that man, and have no company with him, that he may be ashamed. ¹⁵ Yet count him not as an enemy, but admonish him as a brother. ¹⁶ Now the Lord of peace himself give you peace always by all means. The Lord be with you all.

A command at the end of a letter is the concluding thought, focusing in all of the most important messages contained in the letter. Here, Paul is reminding us to keep away from those who are trying to use faith to exploit others. There is an old adage that says if you have to tell people that you are a Christian, you probably are not one. If you have to tell people that you are a Mason, they cannot see from your life, then you joined an organization to carry

2 Thessalonians 3:6-16

a card, not to change your life and help transform yourself into a servant of the Most High God.

Then, as now, some people will try to use a church, or a lodge, or any other organization to advance themselves at other people's expense. Some will say that they are doing the most important work so should have the best resources without being able to show results of what they are doing. Others are going to use the interpersonal dynamics to forget their own pain by causing pain among other, stirring up trouble. We should only have a noble competition of emulating the best characteristics of each other and living in the fullest the *imago dei*, the image of God in which we were made.

There are times in the church or in a lodge when we need to excommunicate someone. This passage reminds us that this is not to hurt that person, but to help them see why they need to be in the organization. The point is to get them back, and for the right reasons. The purpose of the church is to help those who are not members, and the Lodge is not much different.

Questions to ask:

- Which of the words, lines, or ideas do you recognize from Masonic Work? (Remember to not write them down)
- How do these words, lines, or ideas take the meaning of the degrees and Masonic work and focus them to help make our lives more fit for the Builder's purpose and be Good Men and Masons?
- How do these words, lines, or ideas build our Faith in the Great Architect of the Universe?
- Which of these words, lines, or ideas OTHER than what is used in your Masonic jurisdiction help you to maintain your integrity and work for peace and justice?

2 Thessalonians 3:6-16

- Discuss how these lines could be misunderstood or taken for other purposes that do not glorify God or help you grow as Masons.

NOTES:

James 1:17-27

[17] Every good thing given and every perfect gift is from above, coming down from the Father of lights, with whom there is no variation or shifting shadow. [18] In the exercise of His will He brought us forth by the word of truth, so that we would be a kind of first fruits among His creatures. [19] *This* you know, my beloved brethren. But everyone must be quick to hear, slow to speak *and* slow to anger; [20] for the anger of man does not achieve the righteousness of God. [21] Therefore, putting aside all filthiness and *all* that remains of wickedness, in humility receive the word implanted, which is able to save your souls. [22] But prove yourselves doers of the word, and not merely hearers who delude themselves. [23] For if anyone is a hearer of the word and not a doer, he is like a man who looks at his natural face in a mirror; [24] for *once* he has looked at himself and gone away, he has immediately forgotten what kind of person he was. [25] But one who looks intently at the perfect law, the *law* of liberty, and abides by it, not having become a forgetful hearer but an effectual doer, this man will be blessed in what he does. [26] If anyone thinks himself to be religious, and yet does not bridle his tongue but deceives his *own* heart, this man's religion is worthless. [27] Pure and undefiled religion in the sight of *our* God and Father is this: to visit orphans and widows in their distress, *and* to keep oneself unstained by the world.

James is telling his readers to circumscribe their passions and exercise humility and selflessness. We should not be hypocrites who talk a good game, but faithful believers whose belief is so strong that it shows forth in our

James 1:17-27

lives. A helpful way of thinking of this is the Chorister's Prayer from the Royal School of Church Music:

> Bless, O Lord, us Thy servants who minister in Thy temple.
> Grant that what we sing with our lips we may believe in our hearts,
> and what we believe in our hearts we may show forth in our lives.
> Through Jesus Christ our Lord. Amen.

It should come as no surprise to Masons that the bible calls us to aid and assist Widows and Orphans in their distress. There is also no surprise at the admonition to be quick to listen to one another, slow to speak, and slow to anger. When we anger quickly, it is more a sign of a problem in our lives than in any one circumstance. The beginning of this section is thought to be from an early hymn, and as such helps us remember that all gifts from God are worthy of singing His praises. There are no circumstances un life where God is causing bad things in our lives—that is our own doing—God is providing us with opportunity to learn and do, whether we do the right thing or not.

If we look at verse 25, we are asked to see the law of liberty, and contemplate what liberty truly is. Liberty is the freedom to be in and with God, worshipping fully and freely, not under the tyranny of self and the oppression of sin, especially that of selfishness. To be a doer, not a talker, means that we do not seek credit, except thanks that go to God, not to us (see Psalm 115). This idea is taken farther in verse 26, wherein we find yet another reference to the truth of God has to be in our hearts. No matter what we say or what we do, if it is not for God's glory, it is for naught. If we secretly desire praise and glory for ourselves, we are not worshipping God, but trying to remake God in our own image. This is where any religion can go wrong, where

James 1:17-27

people use the faith of others and the Name of God as a weapon to enforce others do our will instead of God's will.

The stains of the world are those corruptions of self-aggrandizement and inflation. If we consider that word inflated for a moment, as it appears in so many of the apostle Paul's writings, the word *phusioó* (φυσιόω) means air-bellows, but the way that Paul uses it means swollen up like a corpse, full of corruption and gas. This is a closer image to what James is referring to here in these ideas of deceiving our own hearts-- we are full of corruption in trying to get ahead and be more admired, to have more jewels on our breasts and better titles. If we exercise true religion, we are focused on God and His creation instead of only ourselves. We follow His commands, not our own selfish desires.

Questions to ask:
- Which of the words, lines, or ideas do you recognize from Masonic Work? (Remember to not write them down)
- How do these words, lines, or ideas take the meaning of the degrees and Masonic work and focus them to help make our lives more fit for the Builder's purpose and be Good Men and Masons?
- How do these words, lines, or ideas build our Faith in the Great Architect of the Universe?
- Which of these words, lines, or ideas OTHER than what is used in your Masonic jurisdiction help you to maintain your integrity and work for peace and justice?
- Discuss how these lines could be misunderstood or taken for other purposes that do not glorify God or help you grow as Masons.

NOTES:

1 Peter 2:4-12

⁴To whom coming, as unto a living stone, disallowed indeed of men, but chosen of God, and precious, ⁵Ye also, as lively stones, are built up a spiritual house, an holy priesthood, to offer up spiritual sacrifices, acceptable to God by Jesus Christ. ⁶Wherefore also it is contained in the scripture,

> Behold, I lay in Sion a chief corner stone, elect, precious: and he that believeth on him shall not be confounded.

⁷Unto you therefore which believe he is precious: but unto them which be disobedient,

> the stone which the builders disallowed, the same is made the head of the corner,

⁸And

> a stone of stumbling, and a rock of offence, even to them which stumble at the word, being disobedient: whereunto also they were appointed.

⁹But ye are a chosen generation, a royal priesthood, an holy nation, a peculiar people; that ye should shew forth the praises of him who hath called you out of darkness into his marvellous light: ¹⁰Which in time past were not a people, but are now the people of God: which had not obtained mercy, but now have obtained mercy. ¹¹Dearly beloved, I beseech you as strangers and pilgrims, abstain from fleshly lusts, which war against the soul; ¹²Having your

1 Peter 2:4-12

conversation honest among the Gentiles: that, whereas they speak against you as evildoers, they may by your good works, which they shall behold, glorify God in the day of visitation.

    The word used in this section is not *petros*, stone directly from the ground, but *lithos*, hewn stone fit for a purpose. This is used to show that it is an analogy, not simply a discussion of building techniques. Living stones are constantly reshaped to be better fit for the builder's purpose. A builder throws away a stone that does not fit his intentions, but God is the real builder. When we reject someone, we think that they do not fit our plans, but this passage reminds us that we are not the builders that matter. It is God who is shaping us to fit His plans. What are the actions that make us more fit, changing us from rough ashlars to living stones that fit perfectly to God's plans?

    The reference to Isaiah 28:14-22 that appears in v.6 is to remind people that no matter what lies we tell ourselves or each other, God's word is like the very foundation of the earth, and it does not crack nor crumble, and is forever. If we are living stones built upon such a foundation, we become a part of that foundation, as it is what we rely on and do not change from.

    Verse 7 opens up a lot of cross-references, especially Psalm 118:22, Matthew 21:42, Mark 12:10, Luke 20:17, and Ephesians 2:20. When we try to focus our desires above God's we tend to make the greatest mistakes. It is also difficult if we think that God only makes the rainbows and the happy puppies. Zechariah 10:4 tells us that: "Out of him came forth the corner, out of him the nail, out of him the battle bow, out of him every oppressor together." The choices that we make are reflections of our hearts. Are our hearts pointed to good or evil? If we are to be the stones which help build up the household of God, we must focus on being strong and well formed, not defective with cracks and holes in ourselves. Society sometimes rejects the best

1 Peter 2:4-12

people because they are inconvenient, or they disrupt the comfortable or profitable. What is right is right, and the other considerations are less important. Peter is reminding us that Jesus was rejected because he was radical in his love, and he did not play by all of the societal rules. We too should be radical in our love and kindness, building each other up and making society better.

Questions to ask:
- Which of the words, lines, or ideas do you recognize from Masonic Work? (Remember to not write them down)
- How do these words, lines, or ideas take the meaning of the degrees and Masonic work and focus them to help make our lives more fit for the Builder's purpose and be Good Men and Masons?
- How do these words, lines, or ideas build our Faith in the Great Architect of the Universe?
- Which of these words, lines, or ideas OTHER than what is used in your Masonic jurisdiction help you to maintain your integrity and work for peace and justice?
- Discuss how these lines could be misunderstood or taken for other purposes that do not glorify God or help you grow as Masons.

NOTES:

Revelation 2:12-17

¹²And to the angel of the church in Pergamos write; These things saith he which hath the sharp sword with two edges; ¹³I know thy works, and where thou dwellest, even where Satan's seat is: and thou holdest fast my name, and hast not denied my faith, even in those days wherein Antipas was my faithful martyr, who was slain among you, where Satan dwelleth. ¹⁴But I have a few things against thee, because thou hast there them that hold the doctrine of Balaam, who taught Balac to cast a stumblingblock before the children of Israel, to eat things sacrificed unto idols, and to commit fornication. ¹⁵So hast thou also them that hold the doctrine of the Nicolaitans, which thing I hate. ¹⁶Repent; or else I will come unto thee quickly, and will fight against them with the sword of my mouth. ¹⁷He that hath an ear, let him hear what the Spirit saith unto the churches; To him that overcometh will I give to eat of the hidden manna, and will give him a white stone, and in the stone a new name written, which no man knoweth saving he that receiveth it.

There is poetry here in the use of the term angel- an angel is one who carries the message of God, so here this means the minister at that church. The Word of God is sharp and can cut sinners or saints if someone tries to abuse it or use it for personal gain as so often happens. Some people join the church because they fall in love with the idea of Jesus, and then become disenchanted when the church is not a collection of magic tricks that can entertain them. If someone cannot have the power, or they think they know better than God what God can do, they leave, losing that

Revelation 2:12-17

first love. Some will go so far as to try and cause other people to stumble. This same type of action can happen in Lodge, where someone does not get an office or honor that he thinks he deserves, or is lazy and unwilling to learn, or so insecure in their faith that they are afraid to be respectful of others' faiths, and so they try to tell the world lies about the Lodge. Truth will set them free...

Verse 17 discusses the 'hidden manna," which most would agree is concerning the true food from God, which is the scriptures. This is occasionally described as the pot of manna inside the ark (see exodus 16:33 and Hebrews 9:4), but this is unlikely. **Hidden** is the hard term here, as most people do not get the idea that it is hidden in plain sight. There is nothing needed for salvation that is not in the Holy Bible, yet people will search high and low for some special information from gurus or charlatans. Among the most contentious parts of Revelation is the discussion of the white stone in that same verse. No one really knows for sure what this means, but it might refer to a practice that the Roman emperors had of throwing out white stones that allowed the bearer of the stone to make a request of the emperor. This is still not that sure an answer, as God provides love and mercy to all who seek Him.

Questions to ask:
- Which of the words, lines, or ideas do you recognize from Masonic Work? (Remember to not write them down)
- How do these words, lines, or ideas take the meaning of the degrees and Masonic work and focus them to help make our lives more fit for the Builder's purpose and be Good Men and Masons?
- How do these words, lines, or ideas build our Faith in the Great Architect of the Universe?

Revelation 2:12-17

- Which of these words, lines, or ideas OTHER than what is used in your Masonic jurisdiction help you to maintain your integrity and work for peace and justice?
- Discuss how these lines could be misunderstood or taken for other purposes that do not glorify God or help you grow as Masons.

NOTES:

Revelation 21:4-6

⁴ And God shall wipe away all tears from their eyes; and there shall be no more death, neither sorrow, nor crying, neither shall there be any more pain: for the former things are passed away. ⁵ And he that sat upon the throne said, Behold, I make all things new. And he said unto me, Write: for these words are true and faithful. ⁶ And he said unto me, It is done. I am Alpha and Omega, the beginning and the end. I will give unto him that is athirst of the fountain of the water of life freely.

While this is among the most beautiful pieces of poetry ever written, it is also among the most profound messages, even in the Bible. The nurturing love of God is so overwhelming that it is hard to comprehend the Creator of the Universe as bending down as a gentle father to wipe away our tears as he would a beloved child. Yet, indeed, that is the image and the reality of how much God loves us. This is Truth, and this encompasses all things, that in God's Kingdom there is nothing bad, as all is made new. Just as the universe was created by God's Word, so too will it be remade in perfection. The reference to Alpha and Omega is that God is the beginning and end of all things. For Christians, Jesus is the incarnation of this image, as He is coeternal and of the same substance as the Father.

Jesus is Truth, and not just any truth, but real truth. Real truth in Hebrew is *'emet* (אֱמֶת pronounced *eh-MEHT*).[13] Truth therefore starts with the first letter of the alphabet, the middle letter of the word is the middle letter of the alphabet, and the last letter is the last letter of the alphabet. The truth of God, like God Himself, is all encompassing.

---

[13] See the section on Esdras above

Revelation 21:4-6

God was, is, and will ever be. Truth is not something that we can change, and relative truth is never the same as Truth given by God. This is why life itself is different in and with God. Truth heals and makes better, just as we are promised, and God will complete humanity is the new Eden, from which living water of His love always flows.

Questions to ask:
- Which of the words, lines, or ideas do you recognize from Masonic Work? (Remember to not write them down)
- How do these words, lines, or ideas take the meaning of the degrees and Masonic work and focus them to help make our lives more fit for the Builder's purpose and be Good Men and Masons?
- How do these words, lines, or ideas build our Faith in the Great Architect of the Universe?
- Which of these words, lines, or ideas OTHER than what is used in your Masonic jurisdiction help you to maintain your integrity and work for peace and justice?
- Discuss how these lines could be misunderstood or taken for other purposes that do not glorify God or help you grow as Masons.

NOTES:

Bible and Masonic Traditions

St. John The Baptist and Masonic Tradition

Saint John the Baptist is one of our patrons because he was a shining example of humility, devotion to God, and of truly loving God. Dalcho said "the stern integrity of Saint John the Baptist, which induced him to forego every minor consideration in discharging the obligations he owed to God; the unshaken firmness with which he met martyrdom rather than betray his duty to his Master; his steady reproval of vice, and continued preaching of repentance and virtue make him a fit patron of the Masonic institution" (*Ahiman Rezon,* p. 150).

Now, it is important to note right off the bat that John was a prophet who Baptized. He was not a Baptist in the modern sense of the word, a denomination that was started in 1609 as result of a split within the Church of England. John baptized people as a continuation of the long Jewish tradition of baptizing to wash away sins and start afresh with repentance. To Christians, Baptism is the outward washing symbolizing inward regeneration by the Holy Spirit. To Jews, the long tradition of Baptism was of repentance and renewed humility. The Hebrew words for Baptism appear in many masonic writings, such as in Psalm 133, which discusses the Dew of Hermon, which descended-- *šeyōréd* - שֶׁיּוֹרֵד -- is a term for Baptism. The reminders through scripture are there to help us remember that while we sin, God forgives, but we must repent and worship God. *Baptizo,* according to Arndt and Gingrich's lexicon, has a range of meanings: "dip, immerse, dip oneself, wash, plunge, sink, drench, overwhelm."

John is not a character that is taken lightly in scripture. He is spoken of in all four of the gospels, as well as in the accounts of Josephus, a famous Roman Jew and 1st-century historian. John was Jesus' cousin, three months

St. John The Baptist and Masonic Tradition older than Christ. John also died a few months before Christ. John is perhaps best-known for being the man who reluctantly baptized Jesus, thereby inaugurating Christ's earthly ministry. John was an important scriptural personality beyond this, as he was a prophet with a special message and a distinct band of disciples with a mission of preparation and repentance.

John is sometimes, unfortunately, thought of as only preaching against the wealthy, against the powerful, and against the leaders of society, calling them a "brood of vipers." It was not against wealth that he preached, but rather he called people to accountability before God. It was against hypocrisy and arrogant self-centeredness that he preached.

John the Baptist was born through the intercession of God. Elizabeth was too old to bear children, but loved God and trusted in Him. Zechariah was a rural priest whose life was devoted to God and serving God's people, and was among a group of people who often ran afoul of the Jerusalem hierarchy, the Sadducees. The Angel Gabriel visited Elizabeth and Zachariah to tell them they would have a son and that they should name him John. Zachariah was skeptical and for this he was rendered mute until the time his son was born and named John, in fulfillment of God's will.

John means *the grace or mercy of the Lord*. It is interesting to note that Elizabeth is a name with many meanings- literally it means *God has built me unto a house*," but we translate it as "God has promised" or "God has established a relationship with me." Zechariah means "memory of the Lord."

When Elizabeth was pregnant with John, she was visited by Mary, and John leapt in her womb. This revealed to Elizabeth that the child Mary carried was to be the Son of God. This may not sound special to us now, but this was a huge event in these terms, as life was not thought to begin until the first breath was taken, the divine "*ruach*"—breath,

St. John The Baptist and Masonic Tradition

spirit, soul, thought, wind-- of God. This may sound strange to our modern ears, but remember that what John was preaching about was that we need to hear scripture in context, and when he preached Isaiah, he was talking about new times that people could not conceive of.

John began public ministry around 30 AD, and was known for attracting large crowds across the province of Judaea and around the Jordan River. Listen, if you would, to the Gospel according to St. ***Matthew 3:13-17 (NIV)***

> [13] Then Jesus came from Galilee to the Jordan to be baptized by John. [14] But John tried to deter him, saying, "I need to be baptized by you, and do you come to me?"
> [15] Jesus replied, "Let it be so now; it is proper for us to do this to fulfill all righteousness." Then John consented.
> [16] As soon as Jesus was baptized, he went up out of the water. At that moment heaven was opened, and he saw the Spirit of God descending like a dove and alighting on him. [17] And a voice from heaven said, "This is my Son, whom I love; with him I am well pleased."

This is the first great reason that John is a patron saint of Freemasonry: Humility. John was a humble man, in the best sense of the word. He preached a strong message, but he never confused himself with the one who had called him. When Jesus approached John for baptism, John hesitated, saying, "I need to be baptized by you, and yet you come to me?" This was no show of false humility. John recognized Jesus, and questioned his own fitness as the one who was being asked to baptize the Son of God. A man of false humility would have continued to protest, declaring his unworthiness in a way designed to elicit praise for such humble behavior. But John didn't argue with Jesus. He didn't protest. Instead, he quietly acquiesced when Jesus explained that this was proper and would serve

St. John The Baptist and Masonic Tradition
to fulfill all righteousness (Mt 3:13-15). John was a humble man, who was able to put his own interests aside when he saw that there was a greater good to be gained by doing so.

John preached a message of repentance. Now, repentance means more than just saying that you're sorry. The Greek word for repentance, *metanoia*, means to turn around, and John begged and urged those who listened to turn towards God from their stray paths, as if urging people to not step off a cliff, but to turn around and be safe. He wanted their words and deeds to follow God, the bear fruits of their thoughts and deeds that glorified God and built God's Kingdom. He led by example, as a wilderness preacher who strictly followed the Law, not out of requirement, but out of Love. He understood that the Law was there to set humanity free from sin, and lived without hypocrisy.

This is the second reason that John is a patron of Freemasonry: he was fully devoted to God. His life's work was carried out in accordance with God's will and in response to God's call. Living life in this way didn't exactly make John a popular guy. He was an outsider from the beginning until the end.

And we know from our own experiences today, that living in accordance with God's will and purpose is not always easy. We are ostracized by society for trying to serve God. We live in a culture that says "Serve yourself!" Self-gratification and entitlement based on one's desires are far more important to this world than devotion to God. To put others before oneself is considered stupid, and giving up individual gain to benefit people who are often complete strangers is thought crazy outside of Freemasonry. It means living your obligations and vows before the Most High God, not in front of other people. Consider, for example, this statement from **1 Corinthians 1:**

[18] For the message of the cross is foolishness to those who are perishing, but to us who are being saved it is the power of God. [19] For it is written:

"I will destroy the wisdom of the wise;
the intelligence of the intelligent I will frustrate."

[20] Where is the wise person? Where is the teacher of the law? Where is the philosopher of this age? Has not God made foolish the wisdom of the world? [21] For since in the wisdom of God the world through its wisdom did not know him, God was pleased through the foolishness of what was preached to save those who believe. [22] Jews demand signs and Greeks look for wisdom, [23] but we preach Christ crucified: a stumbling block to Jews and foolishness to Gentiles, [24] but to those whom God has called, both Jews and Greeks, Christ the power of God and the wisdom of God.[25] For the foolishness of God is wiser than human wisdom, and the weakness of God is stronger than human strength.

Finally, the third great reason was that John is a patron of Freemasonry: he was a man who loved God. Everything about John came from his love of God. His devotion, and humility, and dedication to his call, all belonged to God. He was faithful, even unto death. He told the Sadducees and King Herod, in so many words, that they could take his life, but not his faith and integrity.

Josephus writes about John "who was a good man, and commanded the Jews to exercise virtue, both as to righteousness towards one another, and piety towards God, and so to come to baptism; for that the washing would be acceptable to him, if they made use of it, not in order to the putting away of some sins but for the purification of the body; supposing still that the soul was thoroughly purified beforehand by righteousness. Now when others came in crowds about him, for they were very greatly moved by hearing his words, Herod, who feared lest the great influence John had over the people might put it into his power and inclination to raise a rebellion" (18th Book of the Jewish Antiquities, ch. 5). This gives us a view of John as a revolutionary speaking out against Herod's right too rule as well as the Roman government which was quite common at the time Josephus also states that the Jews believed that the destruction of Herod's army was caused by God for this murder. Freemasons have been known to cause a revolution or two, and a few countries like ours and France owe their existence to Masons and Masonic ideals. Sometimes we even forget that there are countries like Bolivia named after famous freemasons whose love of the Craft led them to help other oppressed people to revolt against unjust rule.

John the Baptist spoke a timeless message of repentance, humility, devotion and love of God transcends time and culture. St. John the Baptist was a man whose life exemplified duty to God through his faith, his religious practices, and through the very living of his life.

Joseph Fort Newton once said, "Righteousness and Love -- those two words do not fall short of telling the whole duty of a man and a Mason." And Masons around the world could do no better in their choice of a patron and a model for living than they have in John the Baptist: a man whose life continues to shine as an example to us all.

NOTES:

St. John The Evangelist and Masonic Tradition

John the Evangelist was also known as the Beloved Disciple. He was the only one of the original twelve disciples to die of natural causes, even if under house arrest on the island of Patmos.

John the Evangelist was a son of Zebedee and Salome, and a brother of the elder James, who became the first martyr of the apostles. He probably grew up in Bethsaida in Galilee and was a fisherman (mark 1:19-20) like Peter, Andrew, and Philip. John was probably about ten years younger than Jesus, and lived until the reign of Trajan (c. AD 98). This means that he was likely over ninety years old when he died. The name John, from the Hebrew חנן (*hanan*), means *God is gracious*. It has been suggested that his name can also be considered to be *beloved* as well as *gracious*, thus rendered *the disciple whom Jesus loved* (See John 13:23; 19:26; 20:2; 21:7, 20). John was considered the Beloved Disciple, and is the one that scripture infers that we as believers should emulate.

John is the beloved disciple who is trustworthy and does things properly. John is found in locations indicating his loyalty to Jesus (John 18:15-18, 19:26-27). He is the one who believes and responds appropriately at the empty tomb, even when he admits that he does not understand (John 20:3-8), but then recognizes the risen Jesus from a distance while the other disciples don't (John 21:7). Many believers think of John as Jesus' bosom buddy because of his leaning back on Jesus' breast in John 13:25, which in Greek is the same phrase *close to the Father's heart* (John 1:18) that is used to describe Jesus' relationship to the Father.

John's mother also followed Jesus and supported him (c.f., Luke 8:3), who purchased spices to embalm him, who were the last at the cross and the first at the open tomb

St. John The Evangelist and Masonic Tradition
(c.f., Mark 15:40-16:11; and Jesus trusted enough to give the care of his own mother to John on the cross (John 19:27).

While Peter laid the foundation of the church and Paul built some of the superstructure, John added the components of the spiritual that were needed for the church to be than a political-religious reform movement within Judaism. John wrote five books of the Bible: the Gospel and three Epistles that bear his name, and the Book of the Revelation of Jesus Christ according to John.

One description of the writings of John are that they are shallow enough for a baby to wade in, and deep enough for an elephant to drown in. These are not the easy, straight forward lessons, but focused and philosophical analyses of Jesus and the Love of God.

Just as John the Baptist was direct and blunt, John the Evangelist was also direct, but he was not always blunt. He was gentle and tried in his writing to get you to love Christ as he loved Christ.

So John the Evangelist became one of Freemasonry's patron saints, even though operative masons already had St. Elizabeth as a patron saint, and Architects had St. Thomas. Why? As mentioned above, he is the apostle to emulate- duty bound, kind, loving, and willing to take responsibility. What more could you ask for in a brother?

NOTES:

NOTES:

Non-Biblical Material of Interest

This section is included since parts of these (and many other) poems are used in several traditions and jurisdictions, either in the degrees, lectures, or regular work of lodges.

William Shakespeare

Hamlet—Act 3, Scene 1:

> For who would bear the whips and scorns of time,
> Th' oppressor's wrong, the proud man's contumely,
> The pangs of despised love, the law's delay,
> The insolence of office, and the spurns
> That patient merit of th' unworthy takes,
> When he himself might his quietus make
> With a bare bodkin? Who would fardels bear,
> To grunt and sweat under a weary life,
> But that the dread of something after death,
> The undiscovered country from whose bourn
> No traveler returns, puzzles the will
> And makes us rather bear those ills we have
> Than fly to others that we know not of?
> Thus conscience does make cowards of us all,
> And thus the native hue of resolution
> Is sicklied o'er with the pale cast of thought,
> And enterprises of great pith and moment
> With this regard their currents turn awry,
> And lose the name of action.—Soft you now,
> The fair Ophelia!—Nymph, in thy orisons
> Be all my sins remembered.

To help delve into this passage that is heard so often, it might help to read it in a modern English translation, here from the SparkNotes[14] website:

> After all, who would put up with all life's humiliations—the abuse from superiors, the insults of arrogant men, the pangs of unrequited love, the inefficiency of the legal system, the rudeness of people in office, and

---

[14] http://nfs.sparknotes.com/hamlet/page_140.html

> William Shakespeare
> the mistreatment good people have to take from bad—when you could simply take out your knife and call it quits? Who would choose to grunt and sweat through an exhausting life, unless they were afraid of something dreadful after death, the undiscovered country from which no visitor returns, which we wonder about without getting any answers from and which makes us stick to the evils we know rather than rush off to seek the ones we don't? Fear of death makes us all cowards, and our natural boldness becomes weak with too much thinking. Actions that should be carried out at once get misdirected, and stop being actions at all. But shh, here comes the beautiful Ophelia. Pretty lady, please remember me when you pray.

In the era of the late 1500s to early 1600s, lands were opening up to discovery, and in which there were either great rewards or great tribulations. Many were proclaiming that the new lands in the Americas and the Far East were rich with opportunity, and sometimes people were shown amazing riches from those lands. Others left for those lands never to be heard from again. Quickly this became symbolized as an issue of faith, and religion became metaphoric back and forth with foreign exploration. Travel, like what awaits us after this life, was a mystery.

Death is the most mysterious aspect of life. In spite of our fascination with people returning from the grave, none has done that except for Christ. Our lives often revolve around death and our fear of it. Our personalities, hobbies, habits, and even our faith systems revolve around avoiding the ill consequences of death. This revolving around death is why this excerpt from Hamlet matters to us.

William Shakespeare

It says what many of us cannot. Ophelia, whose name means "help," goes crazy as she is trying to deal with the issues of life. Her insanity is partly because she is not focused on the greater issues of life- she is help without faith in God. There is always a hope for an undiscovered country that is so amazing that you do not want to go and come back, but that you want to stay and never return. Heaven awaits those whose faith is well founded in God, whose Kingdom is perfect, and no one would want to return from.

NOTES:

Alexander Pope

An Essay on Man: Epistle IV-- Of the nature and state of Man with respect to Happiness

VI. 'But sometimes Virtue starves while Vice is fed.'
What then? is the reward of virtue bread?   *150*
That vice may merit; 't is the price of toil;
The knave deserves it when he tills the soil,
The knave deserves it when he tempts the main,
Where Folly fights for kings or dives for gain.
The good man may be weak, be indolent;   *155*
Nor is his claim to plenty but content.
But grant him riches, your demand is o'er.
'No: shall the good want health, the good want power?'
Add health and power, and every earthly thing.
'Why bounded power? why private? why no king?   *160*
Nay, why external for internal giv'n?
Why is not man a God, and earth a Heav'n?'
Who ask and reason thus will scarce conceive
God gives enough while he has more to give:
Immense the power, immense were the demand;   *165*
Say at what part of Nature will they stand?
  What nothing earthly gives or can destroy,
The soul's calm sunshine and the heartfelt joy,
Is Virtue's prize. A better would you fix?

Then give humility a coach and six, 170
Justice a conqueror's sword, or truth a gown,
Or public spirit its great cure, a crown.
Weak, foolish man! will Heav'n reward us there
With the same trash mad mortals wish for here?
The boy and man an individual makes, 175
Yet sigh'st thou now for apples and for cakes?
Go, like the Indian, in another life
Expect thy dog, thy bottle, and thy wife;
As well as dream such trifles are assign'd,
As toys and empires, for a godlike mind: 180
Rewards, that either would to Virtue bring
No joy, or be destructive of the thing:
How oft by these at sixty are undone
The virtues of a saint at twenty-one!

  To whom can Riches give repute or trust, 185
Content or pleasure, but the good and just?
Judges and senates have been bought for gold,
Esteem and Love were never to be sold.
O fool! to think God hates the worthy mind,
The lover and the love of humankind, 190
Whose life is healthful, and whose conscience clear,
Because he wants a thousand pounds a year.
Honour and shame from no condition rise;
Act well your part: there all the honour lies.
Fortune in men has some small diff'rence made; 195
One flaunts in rags, one flutters in brocade,
The cobbler apron'd, and the parson gown'd;

Alexander Pope

> The friar hooded, and the monarch crown'd.
> 'What differ more,' you cry, 'than crown and cowl?'
> I 'll tell you, friend! a wise man and a fool.   *200*
> You 'll find, if once the monarch acts the monk,
> Or, cobbler-like, the parson will be drunk,
> Worth makes the man, and want of it the fellow,
> The rest is all but leather or prunella.

> Pope, A. (1910). An Essay on Man: Epistle IV-- Of the nature and state of Man with respect to Happiness. In "English Poetry, Volume 40", Charles William Eliot (Ed.). New York: P. F. Collier & Son.

     Pope is here trying to focus the reader on the most important aspects of life, especially virtue. He states clearly that the external goods or qualifications of a person are not what give the person value. If money and tangible goods are the most desired in a person's life, then this can become destructive of virtue. This was a prescient admonition against what is now called the "prosperity Gospel," in which people think that if God loves you, God will bless you with riches instead of with faith and virtue. Faith and virtue cannot be given nor destroyed by earthy things, but only be the heart that dwells on selfishness and sin. If happiness is the end goal of humanity, but happiness is hard to define, yet we know it to be everywhere and at no cost, what are we really doing in life? The greatest philosophers have argued what is happiness, and what is truth. Happiness, according to Poe, is an equalization of hope and fear in spite of your station in life, and this is only available through faith that descends from Heaven.

Alexander Pope
NOTES:

Index

Aaron 37, 42, 76, 142, 143, 148, 159, 160, 161
Aaronic Blessing 42
Abdon 45
Abel 17, 18
Abigail 78
Abital 78
Abraham 23, 27, 29
Absalom 78
Acacia 34
Adonijah 78
Agape 244
Ahasuerus 111
Ahaz 174
Ahinoam 78
Ahiram 82
Aholiab 37
Alamoth 135
Alpha 264
Ammiel 62, 78
Amnon 78
Amorites 27
Apame 202
Apharsathchites 111
Apharsites 111
Appendant Bodies vii, xi
Araunah 64
Archevites 111
Arimathaea 237

ark 31, 37, 94, 160, 262
Ark of the Covenant .65
Artaxerxes 111, 113
Ask, Seek, Knock 217
Asnapper 111
Assur 111
Assyria 173, 185
Baal 45, 154, 155
Babylon 100, 102, 105, 116, 145, 190, 203
Babylonia 204
Babylonians 111, 203
Balaam 261
Baptism 268
Bartacus 202
Bathsheba 61, 62, 78, 79
Beloved Disciple 275
Benaiah 135
Benjamin 23, 104, 111
Bethlehemjudah 48
Bezaleel 37
Bishlam 111, 113

Alexander Pope
Boaz 53, 55, 56, 73, 77, 86
Book of Common Prayer viii, 123, 213
brass 17, 31, 37, 73, 80, 243
breastplate 31
Cabul 82
Caesar 235, 244
Cain 17, 18
calamus 160
Calvin viii, 178
Canaanites 27, 154
candlestick 32, 37, 194, 195, 209
caritas 244
Carmel 78
Chaldees 101
chapter 73, 86
charity 241, 243, 244
chiasm 151
chiastic *See* chiasm
Chilion 48, 50, 55
chisel 69
Christ ix, xi, 6, 59, 121, 131, 178, 238, 240, 244, 247, 251, 258, 269, 272, 276, 281
cinnamon 160
cistern 169
Cleophas 236

Comforter 42
confidence 148, 150
Cranmer viii, 213, 214
Creator 19, 169, 212, 264
Cyrus 101, 104, 105, 107, 111, 116, 203
Dan 22, 24, 25, 37, 81
Daniel 78, 143
Darius 111, 115, 116, 189, 198, 203, 205
David 61, 62, 64, 65, 70, 76, 78, 79, 80, 82, 85, 91, 108, 131, 138, 157, 163, 164
death 11, 14, 49, 52, 98, 120, 123, 149, 151, 171, 186, 201, 233, 244, 264, 272, 280, 281
Dinaites 111
distress 128, 148, 151, 254, 255
Divine Fiat 5
Eglah 78
Egypt 27, 69, 78, 98, 100, 102, 144
eisegeses 182
Eliab 135
Eliada 78
Eliakim 100, 102

Eliam	62		98, 100, 104, 116, 142, 194, 198, 201, 284
Elijah	154, 155	Haggai	115, 189, 192
Elimelech	48, 50, 53, 55, 56	Haggith	78
Eliphelet	78	hammer	69
Elishama	78	heaven	3, 23, 70, 80, 91, 102, 104, 115, 132, 142, 143, 154, 189, 202, 209, 212, 213, 214, 216, 219, 220, 223, 224, 225, 227, 229, 231, 247, 248, 270
Elishua	78		
Elizabeth	269, 294		
Elon	44		
ephod	31		
Ephraim	24, 25, 44, 45		
		Hebron	78
Ephrathites	48, 50	Henadad	108, 109
Eros	244		
Esarhaddon	111	Hermon	159, 268
Ethiopia	198		
Euphrates	98, 116	Herod	272
		Herodian Gate	71
exegesis	182	Hezekiah	174
Ezekiel	25, 82, 143, 180	Hiram	67, 73, 82, 83, 97
Ezra	104, 105, 107, 111, 115, 116, 190	Hittites	27
		Hivites	27
		Hubert Parry	157
firmament	3	Humility	117, 270
forsaken	119		
Gabriel	269		
Galilee	82, 231, 270, 275	Huram	80, 82, 83, 88
		Huram-abi	83, 88
Geshur	78	hypocrite	216
Gilead	44	Ibhar	78
gold	29, 31, 37, 75, 80, 83, 85, 97,	Ibzan	44
		imago dei	252

Alexander Pope
Immanuel 173, 174
India 198
iron 17, 69, 80
Ithream 78
Jabal 17, 18
Jacob 21, 22, 23, 27, 29, 76, 120, 134, 177, 184
Japhia 78
Jebusite 64, 70, 85, 86
Jebusites 27, 70, 71
Jedidiah 61
Jehoahaz 100, 102
Jehoiachin 100
Jehoiakim 100, 102
Jeshua 105, 107, 109, 111, 115, 189, 195
Jesus vi, ix, 53, 109, 125, 209, 212, 220, 229, 231, 232, 233, 235, 238, 240, 251, 258, 260, 261, 264, 268, 270, 275, 276
Jezreel 78
Jonah 210
Joppa 81, 107
Jordan 44, 75, 88, 270
Joseph 22, 23, 24, 45, 237, 238, 273
Josephus 268, 272
Jotham 174
joy 19, 58, 108, 124, 130, 157, 170, 227, 229, 231, 283, 284
Jozadak 107, 109, 115
Jubal 17, 18
Judaea 270
Judah 21, 24, 25, 37, 48, 56, 80, 100, 104, 108, 111, 115, 173, 174, 189, 192, 203
Kadmiel 108, 109
Kedar 176
Kipling 144
Korah 135
Lebanon 80, 97, 107, 203
Levi 21, 24
Levites 104, 107, 180, 204
light vi, 3, 7, 31, 117, 130, 131, 132, 137, 149, 169, 176, 178, 195, 209, 210, 258
lion 21, 25, 97, 120
lithos 259
Love 5, 7, 8, 46, 140, 233, 244, 249, 271, 273, 276, 284
Ludus 244
Luther viii, 134, 224
Maacah 78

Index

Mahershalalhashbaz 173
Mahlon 48, 50, 55
Manasseh 24
manna 261, 262
Mara 49, 51
Mary Magdalene 231, 236
mercy 31, 37, 108, 123, 125, 127, 130, 137, 138, 140, 141, 142, 148, 149, 150, 151, 163, 178, 184, 185, 186, 187, 258, 262, 269
Messiah 150, 152, 178
Micah 138, 187, 210
Midian 27
Mithredath 104, 111, 113
Moab 48, 51, 55
Moriah 70, 85, 86
Moses 27, 29, 31, 33, 37, 42, 62, 107, 138, 160
myrrh 160, 237
Naomi 48, 50, 53, 55
Naphtali 22, 73, 83
Nathan 61, 78

Nebuchadnezzar 100, 104, 116
Nehemiah 76, 105, 190
Nepheg 78
Ninevites 210
Nogah 78
oaths 62, 95
oil 31, 37, 58, 76, 81, 107, 123, 124, 160, 163, 189, 195
Omega 264
Ornan 65, 70, 85, 86
Orpah 48, 51
Parvaim 85
Paul 240, 241, 247, 251, 256, 276
Peace 59, 78, 112, 113, 157
Perizzites 27
Persia 101, 104, 105, 107, 109, 111, 198
Peter 220, 258, 260, 275, 276
petros 259
Pharaoh 27
Philia 244
Philistines 98
Phoenicia 203
Pilate 235, 238
pillar 73, 77
plumbline 184, 185

Alexander Pope

pomegranates	73, 86, 88	Shealtiel	107, 109, 115, 189, 192
portico	69	Shear-jashub	174
Pragma	244	shekel	160
Reformed	178	Shephatiah	78
Rehum	111, 113	Sheshbazzar	104, 105, 116, 117
resurrection	171, 232, 247, 248	Shibboleth	44, 45
		Shimea	78
Reuben	21, 24	Shimshai	111, 113
righteousness	v, 92, 102, 121, 123, 140, 149, 151, 176, 179, 254, 270, 271, 272	shittim	31, 34, 40
		Shobab	78
Ruth	xi, 48, 50, 51, 53, 55, 56	Sibboleth	44, 46
		signet	192
Sadducees	269, 272	Siloam	71
salt	209	silver	29, 31, 37, 40, 64, 76, 80, 97, 100, 104, 116, 142, 169, 201, 204
salvation	22, 24, 46, 94, 130, 131, 135, 148, 149, 151, 190, 224, 262		
		Simeon	21, 76
Salvation	53, 109, 241	*sola fides*	131
		sola gratias	131
Samuel	58, 61, 64, 65, 82	*sola scritura*	131
		Solomon	61, 67, 69, 70, 73, 77, 78, 80, 82, 83, 85, 88, 91, 94, 97, 98
sanctuary	31, 69, 101, 160, 180, 195		
Selah	134	spiritual	v, 53, 56, 131, 138, 170, 178, 212, 248, 258, 276
Septaguint	5		
sepulchre	231, 237	stonesquarers	67
serpent	10, 13, 14, 22, 216	*Storge*	244
		Succoth	75, 88, 89
servant	22, 64, 91, 121, 130, 176, 177, 192, 204, 227, 229, 252	Suffering Servant	121
		Susanchites	111

Tabeel	111, 113
Tabernacle	33, 34, 131, 135
talent	33, 34, 100, 228
Talmai	78
Tamar	56, 78
Tarpelites	111
Temple	34, 38, 50, 61, 65, 67, 70, 79, 82, 94, 105, 108, 113, 116, 131, 135, 154, 195, 203
temptation	124, 212, 213, 214
theophany	95
throne	91, 97, 140, 192, 228, 249, 264
trusted	119, 269
Tubalcain	17, 18, 19
Tyre	73, 80, 82, 83, 107
Uriah	62, 79, 173
Uzziah	174
vanity	166, 169, 170
Vulgate	131, 244
Wycliffe	viii
YHWH	152, 154
Zachariah	269
Zebulun	22, 45
Zechariah	115, 135, 173, 194, 195, 259, 269
Zedekiah	71, 100, 102
Zedekiah's Cave	71
Zeredah	88, 89
Zeredathah	89
Zerubbabel	105, 107, 111, 115, 189, 192, 194, 195, 200, 202, 205
Zidon	22, 107
Ziv	69

About the Author

Rob Elsner, FMR, KCCH, KCT

Dr. Rob Elsner holds academic degrees from the University of North Carolina at Chapel Hill, École Le Cordon Bleu de Paris, the University of Georgia, University College Cork, Virginia Theological Seminary, and Erskine Theological Seminary. A prolific author of scholarly papers, he is on several scientific & medical Editorial Boards and former Editor-in-Chief of *Current Research in Psychology*. Robert is a Licensed Worship Leader and Eucharistic Minister, and has served as a supply preacher at numerous churches in the Upstate of South Carolina.

Robert was initiated, passed, and raised in the time-immemorial First Lodge of Ireland, membership which he will always maintain and cherish. He became a dual member at Old Town Lodge #751 AF&AM in Winston-Salem, NC. , before becoming a plural (and perpetual life) member at Clinton Lodge #3 AFM upon moving to South Carolina. In 2018 he was named District Deputy Grand Master for the 11th District, Commander of the Council of Kadosh for the Greenville Scottish Rite. He served as Right Eminent Grand Commander of the Grand Commandery of Knights Templar of South Carolina in 2018-2019.

When not working or doing Masonic activities, Robert is Scoutmaster of Troop 54, BSA. Governor Nikki Haley appointed him to the Board of the Burton Center for Disabilities and Special Needs, where he has since been elected is Chairman of the Board.

Robert's wife, Elizabeth "Betsy" is from Greensboro, NC, and while they were at UNC together, they did not meet until studying in Paris. They have two adult children: Lily & Sam.

About the Author

NOTES:

Alexander Pope

NOTES:

Made in the USA
Middletown, DE
01 October 2022